You Said Retire & Have Fun.
What's the Problem?

Coy (Buzz) Bozeman

PublishAmerica
Baltimore

© 2007 by Coy (Buzz) Bozeman.
All rights reserved. No part of this book may be reproduced, stored in a retrieval system or transmitted in any form or by any means without the prior written permission of the publishers, except by a reviewer who may quote brief passages in a review to be printed in a newspaper, magazine or journal.

First printing

PublishAmerica has allowed this work to remain exactly as the author intended, verbatim, without editorial input.

ISBN: 1-4241-9538-1
PUBLISHED BY PUBLISHAMERICA, LLLP
www.publishamerica.com
Baltimore

Printed in the United States of America

Thank You

There are several folks that I would sincerely like to thank for inspiring me to put pen to paper and write this book. First, I would like to thank my Mom and Dad for bringing Roy and I into this world. Even though, they were not aware of most of the mischief that we were getting into. I would also like to thank all my sisters for not tattling on us when they knew what we had done, and deserved to be corrected by the Board of Education.

I would like to thank my wife, who heard my brother and the rest of my family tell these stories and never once doubted they were true. I would like to thank my daughter who asked me over and over again to write all these things down so that my grandchildren and great-grandchildren would be able to share in all these events. I would like to thank my youngest son. He sat holding my mother's hand and patting her on the back when Roy and I were talking about some of these things. My Mom was laughing so hard, her face was turning red. My son was afraid she would choke (my mother was partially paralyzed at the time). I would like to thank my son, Mike, who was always supportive of me, as well as his wife, Robin, whom is like a daughter to me. I would like to thank all my grandchildren and great-grandchildren.

I would also like to thank my very best friend in the entire world, without whom, none of these things would have happened: My brother, Roy. I sincerely hope you enjoy reading it as much as I enjoyed writing it.

You Said Retire & Have Fun.
What's the Problem?

Chapter 1

In 1940 and 1941, respectfully, two boys were born to the Bozeman family, Coy and Roy. Immediately these two commenced to rain havoc and terror on everything and everyone in the area, including each other. The boys were inseparable for 17½ years, until Coy entered the navy. A short time later, Roy entered the army. The boys had no contact with each other for about six years. Then short visits and phone calls were their only contact, but they were not close like before.

When Coy and Roy reached their fifties, health problems started to happen. After both had gone through heart bi-pass surgery, they started to visit and call each other more frequently. Coy was a fire fighter with a local fire department and was easy to reach. Roy, being a truck driver, was gone a lot which sometimes made it difficult for Coy to reach him.

Coy had gone to work and was called into the office where the personnel officer, Linda, informed him that they had decided he was no longer fit to be a firefighter. Since they could not depend on him, he was to be retired immediately. His replacement had not only been hired, but was already on duty! After nearly thirty years of dedicated service to this community and department, Coy was devastated. That evening, Coy called upon his old friend and childhood buddy, his brother Roy. The phone rang three times, when Virginia, Roy's wife, answered "Hello?"

"Hi, Virginia, this is Coy. Is Bubba home?"

"Well, hi, Coy! Yes, He is in the bedroom changing his clothes. I will get him for you."

After a short time, Roy answered, "Hi, Bubba! What's going on out there?"

"Well, Roy, they did it to me. After all these years, they really did it to me."

Roy asked, "What did they do to you, Bubba?"

"They put me out to pasture. They actually waited 'til I came to work this morning. They had my replacement already on the job. How could they be so cold? Roy, what am I going to do now?"

Roy replied, "Well, Bubba, why don't you stop sitting there feeling sorry for yourself, you and Maureen pack your bags, and come on back to Oklahoma. We can play some golf, do some sight seeing and we can have us some fun. It will be just like the old times."

"Okie-dokie! Bi-golly, Bubba, I think we will! I really think you have a terrific idea. We will see you guys in a few days."

After talking to his brother, Coy seemed to have mellowed out. He gave Maureen a big smile, he threw his arms around her and gave her a big old sloppy kiss. Maureen was taken by complete surprise. She screamed out gleefully, jumped up from her chair and knocked her cup of coffee off the table. Neither of them seemed to notice the mess on the floor as they embraced.

After calling the children and talking to each of them about their plans, and making arrangements concerning their home and utilities, Coy turned to Maureen and said, "Moe, let's pack our bags! We are on our way to Oklahoma for one of the gosh darndest vacations you have ever seen. Eeehaw! We gonna have us some fun! In fact, let's take that old motor home and take in a few sights on the way.

"Oh, it's going to be the best vacation ever!" Maureen said as she was jumping up and down with glee. She had no idea what lay in store for them in Oklahoma…neither did Coy.

After a few days, the very happy and newly retired couple climbed into their white and green motor home and headed out on their greatest adventure. Coy and Maureen had decided to see some sights along the way. As they were heading east on Highway 140, Coy said, "Honey, did I ever tell you about my Dad's old friend Murray Shultz?"

"No, I don't believe you have."

Coy continued "When we lived on old Bart's place, Murray spent a lot of time at our house. He would come out almost every Friday and he and his family would stay over for the weekend. Murray liked to hunt squirrels. In fact, one Saturday morning, the smell of eggs, coffee and what turned out to be squirrel cooking had aroused me from my sleep. As I came into the kitchen I walked by the stove to see what Murray was frying in the pan. I then decided I was not in the least hungry, and I rapidly headed for the outdoors. I didn't know anyone actually cooked and ate those little squirrel heads!"

"Anyway, my Dad was share cropping for old Bart, at the time. He and another guy, George, each had a team of horses to pull the plows instead of tractors. Every evening Dad would come in from the field, pull the harness off the horses and tie them up to some feed boxes. Then he and old Murray would sit back and tell Roy and me all these stories about ghosts. When they were over seas, the whole country was filled with them. Big ones, little ones, mean ones, scary ones, vampires and some without heads. They would tell us all this junk 'til way after dark."

"Then our loving father, who would never put us in harms way, would say, 'Well, I'm going to go in the house. You boys take these horses down and put them in the pasture. Be sure you fasten the chain on Old King's right foot so he won't jump the fence.'"

"We would look at each other in shear terror. That pasture was about a mile down the road, through thick trees with a lot of brush. Even if the moon was out, you still could not see very far. Besides, if there were ghosts in Germany and England, what would stop them from coming over here? We knew better than to try to argue with our Dad, so we tearfully took the horses and delivered them to the pasture."

"On the way home we walked very close together. Every fiber in our bodies were tense and ready to spring into action with the slightest little noise."

"One of those fateful evenings, old Murray thought he would have himself a little fun. I'm sure good old Dad was in on it. Murray was waiting for us on the way back, hiding behind a tree. When we came up to where he was hiding, he jumped out in front of us with his hands up like a bear, and let out a mighty roar."

"Instead of running away, we were so scared we ran right over the top of Murray! We must have set a record for the mile run back to the house. In fact, we were home and under our beds before anyone even knew we were there."

"It was probably 20 – 30 minutes before old Murray came into the house. He had dirty footprints on the front of his clothes and kind of looked like he had been run over by a truck."

"Mom and Dad started laughing as soon as they saw him. He said his head hurt. When he turned around to show Mom and Dad the bump on his head, everyone started to laugh. Dad said, 'Murray, you might want to go wash up and change your clothes. Your back side is really filthy. It looks like you were dragged in the dirt.'"

"Murray said, 'Yeah, looks like the joke is on me. Those boys should be playing football. I have never been hit so hard in my life! They just ran right over the top of me. Boy, I tell you, I won't ever do that again.'"

The remainder of the trip went pretty well, with stops to see the Grand Canyon, the Yuma prison, and Tombstone. The only problem they encountered was an old Bozeman family problem that Coy suffered from. This problem was called by some, "Foot and Mouth Disease".

Coy and Maureen were having lunch in the non-smoking section of a restaurant packed to capacity. A man walked by their table, puffing on a very large cigar, creating a potent cloud of smoke. Without hesitating, Coy opened his mouth and said, "Hey you!"

The man turned towards him, as Coy continued in a loud voice, "How would you like me to fart right in the middle of your lunch?"

Coffee and sodas were spit across several tables as people started to laugh. From under the table, Maureen, in a very upset tone, stated, "You just embarrassed me to death!"

Coy sheepishly replied, "Well, he got the idea and left didn't he?"

It had been two weeks since Coy and Maureen had left home. They pulled into Roy & Virginia's driveway right around lunch time. As Coy and Maureen were disembarking from the motor home, Roy and Virginia came running out to meet them. After a lot of hugs and yahoos had been passed around, Virginia said, "Hey y'all! Come on in! We have lunch on the table."

While they were eating lunch, Coy and Roy began to reminisce about their childhood and all the crazy things they did as boys growing up in the country. Coy said, "Hey Bubba, do you remember the time we decided to go out in old Bart's pasture and watch them welding and laying the new oil pipeline?"

"Yes. My butt and my head still hurt just thinking about it."

Maureen looked at Virginia and asked, "Have you heard this one?"

Virginia replied, "No, I don't believe I have. Coy, are you going to tell us about it?"

"It was one of those nice warm Saturday mornings. Roy and I were looking for something to do. We remembered the oil company was laying a new pipeline across old Bart's pasture, so we decided to go and watch for a while. We saddled up an old mule and rode out to the pasture. We didn't know that Bart's old jackass, the one he kept in a special lot, had gotten out into the pasture. You see, that old jackass hated other animals, so much so that he would attack and try to kill them. He especially hated the mule we were riding."

"I was in the saddle and Roy was behind me. We were just sitting there watching the welders work, when all of a sudden Roy let out a blood curdling scream. Poor old Toby took off like he had been shot out of a canon. I mean, he took off so fast, we almost flipped off backwards."

"Roy and I were hanging on for dear life. Suddenly, I had a revelation. I saw this tree limb coming at us and I knew in an instant it was barely going to clear the saddle horn. As I was jumping for my life, I yelled at my little brother Roy, 'Jump for your life!'"

"Well, Roy always saw things in a different way than I did. He leaned over the saddle trying to reach the reins. The tree limb was about four inches in diameter and it hit Roy's head dead center. It must have been pretty hard, because it drove him off the back of that mule like a nail. Roy landed on his knees with his face kissing the ground, and his hands and arms outstretched in the position for prayer. The old jack jumped over him at full throttle."

"We didn't have time to nurse our wounds right then because we still had to save our old friend the mule. There were some bones lying near where we hit the ground, so we grabbed up some large bones and took off as fast as we could run. About this time, old Bart came on the scene, caught the old jack and tied him up. Bart also helped us catch our mule and asked, 'Are you ok?'"

"I said, 'Yeah', but Roy said, 'I have a headache my butt hurts where old jack bit me.'"

"I asked Roy, 'Did you say he bit you?' Roy said, 'Yeah, I think he was going after the mule and got me instead.'"

Coy started to laugh and said, "So that's why you screamed like a little girl?"

"Well why don't you just go over there, let him bite you and see how you scream?"

After a few minutes, they were laughing. Roy said, "You know, I think I'm gonna take some time off. Let's go visit all the old the places where we grew up."

"That sounds like a plan, Bubba!"

Virginia said, "Maureen, I think you and I will make our own plans, what do you think?"

"I think that's a good idea. No telling what these guys will get into."

Roy said, "I'm going down to the shop to put in for my vacation right now. Come on, Bubba, you can ride along with me."

"Okay, we can talk about the good old days while we are riding along."

After the boys left, Maureen said to Virginia, "I'm glad you decided to let them have some time together. I think it will do them some good to just relax and have a few laughs." Little did she know what was about to happen.

Chapter 2

After Roy picked up his check and turned in his vacation request, the boys stopped at a small restaurant for pie and coffee. Coy asked Roy, "Say, do you remember that old man out in Pretty Water that raised those really sweet tasting water melons?"

Roy replied, "Oh yeah! Boy, we must have stolen a million of them. I wonder if he is still around."

Coy said, "Yes, we did and we took a few loads of rock salt and kidney beans in the butt from his old shotgun too. I think that just made those melons taste even sweeter don't you?"

Roy leaned back in his chair and gazed up at the ceiling licked his lips and with a sigh said, "Man, I wish we could go back and do it all over again."

"Why don't we do it all over again?"

"Coy, are you nuts?" Roy replied. "Did our momma drop you on your head to many times or something? You know we ain't kids anymore. If he caught us, they would throw us so far back in jail they would have to pipe daylight to us. Or better yet, if that old man shot us with rock salt and kidney beans in the butt with that old shot gun, it would still break us in half."

"Come to think of it, I can't remember the last time I've done anything exiting and daring. Why don't we take a little ride and see if that old fella has any melons in that patch for a couple of real hungry 50+ year old kids?"

Coy said, "Alrighty then, let's get to it."

After a short drive the boys rounded a corner in the Pretty Water community. There it was, the prettiest sight they had seen in years. Five-acres of big green watermelons were just waiting to be carried away by the hungry watermelon burglars.

Roy said, "Coy, it's going to be dark soon, so let's park the truck down by the creek and walk back up the road. I didn't see any dogs, so this will be a snap. He won't even know we are here."

After parking the truck, they walked back up the road. As they approached the melon patch, it was nice and dark. However, they remembered how the old man could see them climbing over the fence in the moonlight, and would get a better shot at them.

The two burglars decided to tunnel under the fence, like they had learned to do when they were kids. They got down on their bellies and started to dig under the fence. It was about this time that the old man who owned the field, following his normal routine, went out behind his house to a kennel and turned his dogs loose. Coy had just broken open a melon and started to enjoy the sweet taste, when the first sounds of terror caught his ears. Very big dogs were on their way to devour the melon thieves.

Coy called out to Roy, "Man, we have been caught! Run for it before those dogs eat us alive!"

Both of them grabbed a melon under each arm and ran as fast as two wanna-be kids again could run. They had just got to the fence when their memories were jogged by a shot gun blast. At the same instant, they were pushed under the fence by a very hot stinging hand of retribution: The rock salt and kidney beans loaded in the shot shells. Fortunately for them, the dogs stopped at the fence.

After some whining and mumbling on both boys part, Roy began scolding Coy. "I told you this would happen. But would you listen to me, noooo! I'm just your little brother! The one you're supposed to take care of! What are we going to tell our wives when we get home?"

Just then Coy noticed Roy still had one perfectly good watermelon, under his arm. Coy pointed to the melon and said, "Hey, Bubba, why don't we just tell them, we went out to a watermelon farm to find just the right one to bring home and serve to the prettiest girls in Oklahoma."

The boys limped down the road laughing. Coy said, "Man, that sure was really something wasn't it?"

"Yeah, but what are we going to tell our wives when they see our butts? I mean let's face it, our butts must look like some really raw hamburger."

The boys walked into the house and placed the melon on the table. Virginia said, "Supper is ready, so y'all come and sit down."

Coy and Roy looked at each other and shrugged. Both boys tried to sit down carefully, but it was apparent to both women that something was wrong and each demanded to know what was going on.

With some attempts to make the story sound better than it was, both boys finally told what had taken place. The two women looked at each other and screamed in unison. "What on God's green earth possessed you two to do something like that?!"

Virginia jumped to her feet, "Roy what were you thinking? You're an old man, not a twelve year old kid."

Maureen, pointing her finger at the end of Coy's nose, screamed, "And you're not a kid either, Buster! You certainly know better. What got into you?"

Roy explained, "Virginia, you know I love you and you know I would never do anything like this. You have to believe me when I say it was all Coy's fault. He made me do it. He is the oldest and I am the little brother, right?"

Virginia and Maureen looked at each other and smirked. Virginia said,

"Roy, you're a grown man. Don't put the blame on Coy. He didn't twist your arm and pull your hair to make you do this."

Roy said, "How do you know? You weren't there!"

Virginia poured coffee for everyone and sat back down at the table. She and Maureen stared at the two old red faced boys for a moment, then looked at each other and burst out laughing. Maureen asked, "Coy, did your family ever do anything to have fun that didn't hurt anybody?"

Coy replied, "Well, sure we did. When we were kids, Dad didn't always have a car, but we always had horses. Mom and Dad bought all their groceries on the first of the month. Dad would harness up the team of horses, hook them up to the old wagon and we would all go to town. Mom would take a special cake that she had baked for the occasion. They would usually buy a whole stick of baloney, some red onions, a big round chunk of longhorn cheese and a loaf of store bought white bread, with some mayonnaise and mustard. They would also buy a case of Nehi sodas."

"On the way home, Dad would find a shady spot along side a creek. While Mom made some very large sandwiches, Dad would cut some tree limbs for all of us to use for fishing poles. Dad always seemed to have fishing line, hooks, and sinkers with him. After eating our lunch, we would all go fishing for a couple of hours. Then we would have a piece of Mom's home baked cake and a second soda before we would head for home. We kids would usually nap the rest of the way home."

Virginia said, "I am glad your family had some normal kinds of fun."

Later that evening in the privacy of their bedrooms, the women gently rubbed antiseptic cream on the very tender butts of their husbands. Meanwhile, they were demanding that they use their heads for something other than a place to hang their hat. The neighbors could still hear the two very unsympathetic wives laughing hysterically.

The next morning, Maureen and Virginia got up early and decided to go play a round of golf, have lunch and do a little shopping. Each of them wrote a note to their husbands, telling them to stay out of trouble, and to try really hard to remember they had a brain and to use it. They each pinned the notes to the bedroom doors at eye level so they could not be missed.

It was after 8:00 am when the boys started stirring around. Roy was in the kitchen when Coy came in. Roy said, "Hey, Bubba. Want some coffee?"

"Yeah, but I think I'm gonna stand to have my coffee and breakfast this morning."

Roy said, "Yeah, me too. You know, Bubba, that old man must be in his nineties at least, but you wouldn't know it the way he spotted and peppered us last night."

"Ah, it was just luck," Coy replied. "He couldn't do it again in a million years."

"Wait a minute! Now just hold onto your britches just one goldarn minute. You're not thinking of going back there are you?"

Coy said, "Not today, but tonight would be fun. After all, we never let him get one up on us when we were kids, did we?"

"No, but we were younger and faster then. Come to think of it, he was to. So what are we going to do tonight, and what are we going to tell Maureen and Virginia?"

"We will tell them we are going to play some night golf," Coy answered. "Now as for that old man, remember how we used to catch up his horses and ride them around his pasture? He would chase us around, waving that old shotgun screaming he was going to shoot us if we didn't get off his horses."

Roy said, "Yeah, but we knew he wouldn't shoot as long as we stayed on his horses. Now if we were dumb enough to get off the horses, he most definitely would pepper our back sides."

"Well, I am feeling the most gosh awful need to go for a midnight horsy ride," Coy said. "What about you?"

"I don't know. That old man will probably catch us and then our wives will probably kill us!" Roy replied.

"Ah, stop your whining. You didn't carry on like this when we were kids. Come on let's go get some stuff for tonight."

A little begrudgingly Roy said, "Ok."

In the mean time, Maureen and Virginia were just coming back into the clubhouse for lunch. Maureen said to Virginia, "I have heard some of these stories about what our husbands did as kids growing up here in Oklahoma. As much as I hate to admit it, I am kind of envious of them. It really sounds like they had a lot of fun growing up."

Virginia said, "Yes, I must agree with you. But I'm not sure I could have gone through with all these things. I really hope those characters are not going to start going through a second childhood. How about you?"

"I guess you're right. I must admit, I'm going to find it awfully hard to keep a straight face and scold them if they get into trouble. We are talking about two little old men here."

"You're so right," Virginia agreed. "Whatever we do, we had better not let their children know about any of this. Those kids would just egg them on. What kind of an example would they be setting for our grandchildren?

Chapter 3

Coy and Roy went down to the local feed and weed store to purchase some needed tack for their upcoming adventure. Roy said "Coy, do you remember that old paint mare of Bidelmans? You know the one that had to be kept in the corral because she was his favorite?"

"Oh yeah, do I ever," Coy started. "In fact, I remember a night that we went for a ride. Dad had Jessie Bartlet come over the day before and ride her till she stopped bucking. Dad told me I had to ride her every day so she would gentle down."

"It was the next night that you and I decided to go for a ride. "You took the old brown horse and I took that paint mare. Everything was going pretty good until we decided to go through that old wooden gate. You got off, opened the gate, led your horse through and held the gate for me to come through when that mare decided to buck. Just as she started to buck in the direction of the gate, I saw your face. It turned a really pale color and your eyes got as big as dinner plates."

"I was holding on for my life after seeing your face. She hit the gate, knocked it down and tapped danced over the top of you. I have to admit, it was hard to hold onto the horse, but it was even harder to not bust out laughing. I think I was chuckling some though. Of course, when it was over and you screamed, 'You animal! You're trying to kill me!' I couldn't contain myself."

Roy said, "Yeah, that was one of those 'you should have seen the funny part' speeches."

"Bubba," Coy said, "We had better pay cash for this stuff or there may be a lot of questions we don't want to be answering."

Roy agreed, "Yep, when you're right, you're right as rain."

The old boys picked out two saddle pads, two bridles, two lead ropes and stashed them behind the seat in Roy's pickup. Just as they were getting in the truck, Coy said, "Whoa, Bubba! Wait a minute. We had better get some sweet smelling grain so them horses will come up to us. We don't want to be chasing them around the pasture. That old man might get in a couple more of them lucky shots."

"Oh, yeah. If he got my backside again tonight, I would be cryin' some mighty big cow type tears when I got home. Virginia would probably whup on both of us for being so stupid."

"Well, Bubba," Coy said. "We had better get on home and take us a nap before those girls get home. We don't want to arouse their suspicions any."

The old boys went home and attempted to sleep, however, the excitement of the upcoming event kept coming to mind. Every few minutes, a chuckle or even a laugh would be heard coming from one of the bedrooms.

Later that evening, Maureen and Virginia arrived home. Coy and Roy were out on the patio barbequing some chicken, joking about their plans for the evening. Virginia asked as she came out on the patio, "What's so funny?"

The boys looked at each other, shrugged and said, "Oh nothing much. We were just talking about the president and cigars."

As they sat down to dinner, the two boys were so excited, they could hardly eat their dinner. Coy asked, "Virginia, did I ever tell you about the first job Roy and I had?"

"No, you didn't," she answered.

Coy continued, "My first job was working for old Bart. I was probably in the third grade. Bart had this old mule named Toby. He had this old push garden plow with one big wheel on the front."

"Bart hooked a single tree on the front of the plow, so that he could hook the harness traces up. That way the old mule could pull it. He then took me out to the field that he had already plowed. That field looked like it was five miles long. Bart showed me how to drive and put the mule down in the furrows. The little plow had to be right down in the center of the furrow."

"Bart told me that he wanted me to subsoil the field for him. He was going to pay me a dollar a day, but he didn't pay me until school started. Roy and I caught the school bus right in front of Bart's house every morning. He would come out and give us biscuits with butter and honey to make sure we had breakfast before school. On Monday mornings he would give us a dollar to pay for our lunches."

"The next year, he hired Roy and me both. That year we were going to feed his hogs all summer, for two dollars a day. It was a real hard job too. We had to take a stick and go around to all the self feeders to poke up holes, and make sure that the feed fell down in the trough."

"Like the year before, he waited 'til school started to pay us for working all summer. In other words, he would give us our lunch money. When we went to feed those pigs, we would just steal a couple of Bart's horses and go for a ride. We thought we were being pretty sneaky, and we didn't think he knew about it. Now that I think back, it was kind of strange. He had a locked tack room where he kept his saddles, harness, and such. However, there were always two bridles hanging on a nail outside the tack room."

"In fact it was one of those mornings that Roy was bucked off for the first time. We had just caught up two sorrel horses, and Roy made me ride the mare to show him how gentle she was. I helped him on her back, but she didn't want to leave the lot. I swatted her rump with a short piece of rope. She walked out of the gate and trotted down to the hog wallow where she started to buck. Roy threw away the reins, locked his arms around her neck and started to go off one side. He then went up the other side of her neck like an airplane propeller. He finally fell off landing flat on his back in the creek. The water was only three or four inches deep, but the hog manure and mud was at least a foot deep. He landed right in front of that old mare and sunk out of sight."

"The mare jumped over him. Roy sat up behind her, wiping the mud out of his eyes, just in time to see her kick back at him. He flopped back down in the mud."

"Being concerned about him, I jumped off my horse and ran down to the creek. He sat up and wiped the goop out of his eyes again. I asked, 'Are you ok little brother?' He answered me with a sarcastic tone, 'You-you animal! You're trying to kill me!' I could not contain myself any longer."

As soon as dinner was over, Coy and Roy were out the door. They jumped in Roy's truck and headed down the road to Pretty Water. Their plans were all worked out. Everything was going to be fantastic. While they were driving along, Roy asked, "Coy, do you remember when we lived on the old Bidelman ranch? When Mom and Dad would leave, we would get that old 9n tractor out of the barn and drive it around."

Coy started to laugh and said, "Oh yeah, in fact, I remember an evening when Mom and Dad left us home. You beat me to the tractor and you had it in high gear spinning donuts in the corral. I kept yelling at you to give me a turn, but you just ignored me, so I yelled out, 'Here comes Dad!' and you drove straight into the fence, knocking it down! Out of the kindness of my heart, I helped you put that fence back up before Mom and Dad came home."

Roy said, "Oh yeah! The kindness of your heart all right. If you had a kind heart you wouldn't have yelled out, 'Here comes Dad!'"

"Hey, mister! If you had been a kind person, you would have let me have a turn! Remember when Mom got us up the next morning to go out and feed the cows?" Coy continued. "When we came into the kitchen, Dad was sitting there looking out the window. It had been raining all night and we knew what he was looking at."

Roy said, "Oh yes, I do and we wouldn't look out the window because we were afraid he would know we did it."

"It was sure hard to swallow that lumpy oatmeal with our hearts in our throats." Coy amused.

"It sure was," Roy agreed. "When he said, 'Ma, I want you to look what that old mare has done to my fence', I could have run right out there and kissed her on her old lips!"

"Yeah me too, cause I just knew he was gonna kill the two of us!"

As they approached the old mans farm, Coy said, "The horses are out in the pasture. We can get to them from the back side so we won't be anywhere near the house."

Roy said, "I just hope we can get on those horses before those dogs figure out we are here."

"Aww, come on now. Don't be such a worry wart. You get those saddle pads and the bridles, I'll get the grain. Let's just mosey on over there ok?"

In the moonlight, the boys could see four horses out toward the center of the pasture. There were lights on in one room of the old mans house and what appeared to be a bluish glow in the window. The boys felt confident that the old man was watching television and probably wouldn't even hear the dogs if they did bark. They boldly walked right on out where no one had gone before.

Coy caught one of the horses. Of course, in the dark, neither he nor Bubba Roy realized they had caught a stud horse. They were in the process of putting the saddle pad on when they heard the dogs coming. Roy, not wanting to be caught on the ground, told Coy, "Throw the saddle pad down and help me on the horse!"

Coy said, "Hey! What about me?"

"Bubba, I am the little brother and you have to take care of me remember?"

"Well ok," Coy conceded as he threw the saddle pads on the ground. Coy helped Roy up on the horse. He then grabbed the saddle pads and one bridle and ran toward the fence as fast as his tired old legs would carry him. Coy was sure a very large Doberman was about to take a mouth full of his sore backside. Instead, he heard the sound of the old 12 gauge shot gun and the terrible sting of rock salt and kidney beans on his very raw butt. The shot rocketed him across the fence in record time.

The sound of that old shot gun in the still night created quite a different story for Roy. Roy wasn't the best rider to begin with, even on a gentle horse. This was not a gentle horse at all. The sound of that old shotgun caused this horse to become the horse from hell. He began to buck, jump, kick and squeal. Roy was fighting for his life. He was holding on to the horse's mane and wrapped his legs around the horse's neck. He then found himself running along side the horse, then he was back on the horse, and finally he was thrown off.

He landed on the ground and suddenly found the horse was coming back after him with his teeth snapping. Roy took off as fast as he could. Just as he was going under the fence, the shotgun found its mark, helping poor Roy to the other side of the fence.

As the boys walked back to the truck, Roy said to Coy, "You know, things never change, do they? Here I have always been such a kind, considerate and loving brother to you. And you, you, you animal! You're always trying to get me killed! Look at me my, my, pants are torn; my, my shirt looks like a rag, and my wife will either kill me or divorce me!"

Coy stuttered, "Well, Roy, I'm. I'm. Huh, huh, ha, ha, ha, hee, hee! I'm sorry, Bubba, but I really wish you could have seen what I saw. I mean, if you could have seen yourself on, or at least almost on, that horse you would be laughing too. That had to be the funniest thing I have ever seen, or at least the funniest thing I have seen in years!"

Roy thought a minute and started to laugh. He said, "I guess it was pretty funny, but just once I would like to be the one to actually see the funny part."

The two old boys walked back to the truck, laughing hysterically. Virginia heard them come into the kitchen. She called out to Maureen, "They're home!"

As the women came into the kitchen, they saw the very dirty, scratched, bruised, old men standing in rags. Both women screamed out in unison, "Wwwhaatt happened to you two?! Was the gang that did that to you arrested?! Please say their not out on the street so they can do this to someone else!"

Roy dropped his head, staring at his feet and said, "Virginia, there was no gang. Me and Coy were just out riding horses, that's all."

Virginia raising her voice to a concerned and very audible level asked, "What kind of horses were you two riding? Was there a rodeo in town that we didn't know about? I've seen people in the hospital emergency room that looked better than you two!"

Virginia looked at Maureen and shrugged her shoulders, then said, "Well, Maureen and I made dessert. Would you two like to have some with us?"

The two old guys asked, "Could we stand to eat it, please?"

Maureen and Virginia looked at each other and Maureen asked, "Don't tell us you went back out to that old man's farm to get even, and you lost again right? Right?"

"Well, yeah," Roy said. "I just don't understand it. That old man must be at least a hundred years old. How can he be so full of vinegar?"

Coy said, "As old as he is, he should be half blind, with one foot on a banana peel and the other in a grave. If I didn't know better, I would think he was younger than we are. I tell you its plumb uncanny."

After having their dessert the two couples went to their rooms. The two very concerned ladies applied more antiseptic cream to the back sides of these 60+ plus year old boys, while assaulting their ears with pleas to grow up and act their age. Stop playing cowboys and Indians and try playing golf, going to the movies or watching TV. Come to your senses and act like respectable old men.

Chapter 4

The next morning the old boys came into the kitchen where Maureen and Virginia were preparing breakfast. Sheepishly Roy asked Virginia, "What's for breakfast this morning?"

Virginia looked at Maureen with a wink and said, "Well, this morning we thought we would have a healthy meal since the two of you probably need more energy to keep up with your childish exploits. In fact, we are having orange juice, prunes and bran flakes."

The boys looked at each other. Coy started to moan and Roy started to beg, "Oh, Virginia. Honey, baby, please have some mercy on us! Could we have some eggs with cheese? Maybe some pancakes and coffee? You know, something sort of binding? After all, we don't want to be loose right now. Sitting down is such a painful experience."

Virginia said, "I hope you think about that before you get into any more trouble, ok?"

"Yeah, but tell that to Coy. It's his fault. It was all his idea, not mine."

Virginia said, "Oh sure. You're just a mindless old fart that can't think for himself and have to be led around by the hand."

"Maureen and I are going out today. I want to show her some of the sights around this area. Now please, I am begging you two to stay out of trouble, ok? Coy, no big ideas ok? Roy, no following around ok?"

Both boys said, "Ok," while looking at the floor.

After the ladies left, the boys were sitting out on the patio having coffee. Each of them were sitting on two bedroom pillows, and were being very careful not to move around. "Well, Bubba," asked Roy. "What do you want to do today? That is, what do you want to do that won't get us bit in the butt today?"

Coy replied, "Well, I was just thinking what a nice warm day it is."

"Yeah," Roy agreed. "When we were kids, on a day like this we would have taken our fishing poles and headed for the creek."

"We would have ended up swimming more than fishing."

Roy said, "Hey, remember that old tree that leaned out over the deep swimming hole?"

"Oh yeah, the one we built the diving platform in. That was the one that Johnny's little brother Tommy was always climbing up there on the platform and threatening to jump. The little pest couldn't even swim. Johnny would beg him to come down before he fell in."

Roy said, "Remember that day we decided we had put up with him one time to many, climbed up there and threw him in?"

Coy said, "Yeah, we were yelling sink or swim. It was kind of funny how he only went down three times before he got the idea that we meant it. He started to swim pretty good after that."

Both boys were laughing. Coy asked, "Remember that day the four of us went fishing, and you and Johnny took off down the creek, leaving me with 'Mr. Pain-in-the-peetute,' Tommy? You know, I was really trying to fish, but he just wanted to annoy me. So, I used his fishing line to hog tie his hands and feet. He kept screaming, so I stuck his old dirty sock in his mouth. Then I was able to enjoy the peace and solitude along with the warm sunshine."

"When the fish stopped biting and I ran into you and Johnny, I realized I forgot all about Tommy. I can still remember the panic we all felt when we remembered him and started looking for him. You and Johnny asked me where I left him. We got back to that little beach and he wasn't there. We looked all over for him, then lucky for him we spotted a little bright red thing floating in the creek."

Roy remembered, "Yeah, his nose was sure sunburned. It must have peeled off at least six or eight layers."

Coy said, "Yeah, but can you imagine being tied up with your hands behind your back and deciding to roll into the water?"

"It was a good thing the water was shallow there."

"You got that right," Coy agreed. "He still had to hold his head up to keep his nose above the water. Boy, we sure did have a lot of fun on that old creek didn't we?"

"We sure did."

"Roy," Coy asked. "I wonder if that old swimming hole is still there."

"Bubba, get your swim trunks and let's get going!"

"Hey, you mean to tell me we are really going to wear suits this time? I don't recall us wearing any suits when we were kids."

Roy said, "Aw, come on. Let's go swimming."

"Wait a minute, Bubba," Coy hesitated. "If I remember correctly, that old swimming hole is right behind that old mans property."

"Yep, in fact, right on top of the old cliff above the swimming hole is where he used to stack his hay for the horses. Come on let's get going."

Grabbing up their suits the two old boys climbed into Roy's truck and headed out to the Pretty Water area again for a little taste of the past. As they were driving along Roy said, "Bubba, remember when you and me and the Bolus boys were swimming down at the creek and camped out for the night?"

"Yeah, you mean the time we decided to steal a chicken from Mr. Brown?"

Roy said, "Yeah, the Bolus boys and me thought you were going to drown trying to swim the creek with that chicken under your arm!"

"I thought I was going to drown too. Then we all came to the conclusion that none of us knew how to cook it in the first place. Besides, none of us had the heart to kill the poor thing."

"Well," Roy continued. "Those ears of corn we got out of the cornfield and roasted over the fire didn't taste too bad."

"I think that old chicken liked our dinner better than we did."

"That sure was embarrassing having to take that old chicken back to Mr. Brown and telling him how sorry I was for stealing her in the first place."

Coy agreed, "You should have been sorry."

"Hey you, wait just a minute. There were four of us that stole that miserable old hen."

"Actually," Coy argued, "You are wrong, it was only you."

"It was not."

"Yes it was. Do you want me to prove it to you?"

Roy challenged him, "Yeah." Roy said yeah.

"Ok, let's go over to the Browns'."

"Oh, yeah right! I see how you are. I took the chicken back and I said I'm sorry, so that means I'm the one that stole the chicken."

Coy said, "Yes, it's a matter of record."

"Yeah, but you seem to have forgot all about drawing straws to see who took that old hen back."

After parking the pickup near the old bridge the brothers headed up the creek bank in search of the old swimming hole. It was a fifteen minute walk to the old swimming hole. There appeared to be a lot of under brush that had grown up over the years, but there was still a small beach right under the cliff at the edge of the old mans property. Looking around, Coy spotted a very rusty piece of cable hanging out of the old tree. Coy said, "Hey, Bubba look up there. Remember the old cable trolley we rigged up across the creek when we were kids?"

Roy looking up at the tree said, "Oh yeah. Remember how we used to put that old pulley wheel with the handles on the cable? We would ride out over the creek, turn loose of the handles and try to do flips or cannon balls before we hit the water.

"Yeah," Coy remembered. "But it seems like our biggest trick was diving down trying to find the trolley. We finally got smart and attached a chain from one handle to the other under the cable, so the trolley didn't fall off."

The sun was warm, the sandy soil felt soft and warm and the water was clear and cool. The old boys were just laying on the sand sun bathing and relaxing. The warm sun felt good on their bruised up old bodies.

After an hour or so had passed, Roy said, "Hey, Bubba, look up there."

Coy asked, "What are we looking at?"

"Those hay stacks. Looks like that old man is still stacking his hay there, just piling it up loose around a pole."

Coy said, "Yeah, it used to be fun climbing up on top of those stacks and sliding down the hay. You had to be watching though, because that old man would sneak up and let you have a big dose of rock salt and kidney beans right in your sliding down part."

"Hey, Bubba, you want to?"

Coy questioned, "Do I want to what?"

"You know what. Come on."

"Oh, yeah right! I say ok, and then if we go up there and get caught, you're gonna say 'it was all Coy's fault. He twisted my arm and dragged me up there by the hair. Heck, he even carried me up the hay stack and jumped in front of me when the old man shot at us.'"

Roy said, "I will not. I ain't never done any such thing before and you know it."

"Well, ok. Let's go then."

The boys found their way up the fourteen or fifteen foot cliff. They made a few slides down the haystack that was closest to the creek. Roy was just starting to slide down again, when Coy shouted, "Hurry, Roy! Jump for the creek! The old man and his dogs are coming."

With that Coy ran and jumped for the creek. After bouncing his way through the under brush and a couple of tree limbs, Coy landed flat on his back in the shallow water at the edge of the creek. Roy slid off the hay and hit the ground running for the edge of the cliff. He reached the edge of the cliff and leaped out into space just as shot gun fired. Luckily, the rock salt just rattled through the brush.

Roy bounced off the tree limbs and under brush, and landed flat on his back in the shallow water next to Coy. Coy looked at Roy and said, "We had better get out of here before that old man catches up with us."

With that, the boys dragged their beaten and battered bodies up and hurried as fast as they could, away from the old man and his demon dogs, to the safety of Roy's truck. All the way home Roy was saying, "Oh, Coy, look at our clothes! Look at our bodies! Bubba, our wives are going to be so mad. What happened? We were just going to go swimming."

Coy said, "I really don't know, Bubba. I think the devil must have made us do it."

As soon as they walked into the house, Virginia was staring at them with very wide eyes and a gaping mouth. Before she could say anything, Roy said in a very humble voice, "It was Coy's fault he. He twisted my arm, dragged me up there by the hair and he even carried me up the hay stack and pushed me off. Then when the old man came after us, he pushed me over the cliff."

Virginia said, "Roy, stop blaming your brother for your actions. You are a big boy."

"Hey, he made me tear my bathing suit and I think I must have broken every bone in my body. Even some bones I didn't know existed."

"My itsy-bitsy wittle bruver," Coy teased. "What happened to 'cross my heart'? I seem to remember saying 'I won't say it was all Coy's fault' or 'I won't say it was Coy's idea,' etc."

Roy apologized, "I'm sorry, Bubba, but it would have been all your idea if you had thought of it first right, right?"

"Well, maybe."

Virginia said, "I don't know what we are going to do with these two."

"I don't know either. I guess we are lucky they haven't gotten into trouble with the law. You haven't, have you Roy? Coy? Come on, tell me the truth. Please promise me you haven't."

Both boys started laughing, "No, we haven't done anything like that. We have just been having some fun that's all."

After dinner the boys and their wives were sitting on the patio having coffee and listening to the radio. Coy sat his coffee cup down, leaned back in his chair and said, "You know, I was just thinking about the time the Bolus boys Mom and sisters decided they wanted to take us to church with them."

Roy said, "Oh yeah, Virginia, you gotta hear this one."

Maureen agreed, "I think I want to hear this one too."

Coy said, "It was a Saturday afternoon. The Bolus boys, Roy and I were out playing down by the creek. We didn't know the Bolus girls had talked to our Mom about their idea of taking us to church with them the next day. They even came down to the house and got our clothes from our Mom."

"Later that evening, they came to our house to get us and take us home to spend the night. The next morning, the girls got their brothers, Roy and I up first and got us ready for church. They sent us outside with instructions to stay out of trouble and to stay clean. They should have known better. Once we were outside, we heard their old beagle hound barking. This dog was so old he didn't have a tooth in his mouth. He had to eat oatmeal with lots of milk."

"Anyway, all us boys ran over to an old wash where the dog had a skunk cornered. The skunk had its head in a hole in the bank of the wash. The dog would run up behind the skunk and bite it in the backside, where upon the skunk would fill the air and the dog with that very pungent spray. After a few minutes, the skunk made a break and ran as fast as it could, to get away. The dog was behind the skunk and four boys were behind the dog. The skunk saw a hole in the ground and dove in. Unfortunately, the hole was an abandoned oil pipe. So the boys all got down, put their ears to the pipe and listened to the skunk travel down the pipe."

"About this time the girls and their mother were getting into the car to leave for church. They called out to the boys, "Come on, we are a little late.""

So the boys all ran up to the car and opened the doors to get in. Mom and the girls threw open the doors on the other side, got out and ran for the house. They screamed at the boys to go play in the creek and not to bring back the clothes."

The two couples were laughing hysterically.

The radio was playing, but it really wasn't turned up that loud. Out of the blue, Roy's neighbor appeared and yelled at Roy, to turn the blankety-blank radio down. It was interfering with his TV. Roy said, "Mr. Jinx, if you don't go and mind your own business, I'm going to shove that fence up where the sun don't shine."

Mr. Jinx disappeared. Coy said, "Hey, Bubba, why don't we get even with that clown?"

"Whoa," Virginia jumped in. "Don't you two go getting yourselves into trouble, you hear."

Roy said with a smirk, "We won't. I think Bubba has an idea and I really want to hear what it is."

"Do you remember when Dad told us how to make people think they were hearing ghosts in the night?"

"Oh yeah," Roy replied. "You mean with the string and a few other things right."

"You bet!"

Roy said to Virginia and Maureen, "Tomorrow night, you are going to see the Jinxs all huddled outside in their jammies."

Virginia said again, "I don't want to see you guys getting yourselves into trouble."

Chapter 5

The next morning, the boys awoke early and excited about their upcoming planned event. In fact, they could hardly contain themselves. As soon as they had finished their breakfast, they were out the door and in Roy's truck, heading into town. Their first stop was a variety store where they picked up some cotton kite string and a 16 penny nail. Then they went to a sporting goods store and picked up some powdered resin. Their last stop was a music store, where they picked up some solid resin used on violin bows.

When they returned home, Roy asked Virginia, "Do you know if the Jinxs are home?"

"Roy, how would I know if they were home or not?"

Coy said, "Roy, why don't you take your cell phone over there and ring their door bell. If they answer, you can keep them busy while I go over there and drive our nail into the end of one of their ceiling rafters. If they are not home, you can call me on the phone and tell me to go drive the nail. Ok?"

"The Jinxs are afraid of me, though. If I go to their door, they won't answer."

"I may have a better idea," Coy said. "Virginia, why don't you and Maureen go to the door. Maybe you could ask to borrow some brown sugar and talk about making some cookies or something to keep them busy."

Virginia hesitated, "Well, I don't know about this."

Roy pleaded, "Aw, come on Honey, please. It's going to be fun and they will never know what happened."

Virginia and Maureen both agreed, as long as they never found out they had anything to do with it. So Maureen and Virginia were off to the Jinxs. Coy and Roy were waiting behind the fence. After about ten minutes, Coy's cell phone rang. It was Virginia saying that no one was home. Hanging up the phone, Coy said, "Ok, Bubba, let's go."

The two old boys slipped over the fence, ran up to the Jinx's house and drove their nail into the end of one of the roof rafters. They tied the end of their kite string tightly around the nail. They were coating the string with a very heavy coat of the powdered resin, before climbing back over the fence.

By this time, it was getting dark. The boys and their wives, sat back quietly having coffee and waiting for the Jinxs to come home. Virginia fixed dinner and the foursome sat down to eat. Looking across the table, Virginia asked, "Roy, tell us what is going to happen?"

"Whoa," Coy stopped them. "Let's not talk about it. There might be some ears listening. Just remember, it will be hysterical."

The foursome returned to the patio to enjoy their coffee and listen to the radio. Coy said, "Roy, do you remember that Christmas, I think it was up in Okmulgee, when we were about ten or eleven years old? It had been raining for several days. We were out in the yard picking up night crawlers and earthworms, while Mom was in the kitchen wrapping some small Christmas presents. She was tying them up with little pieces of string that she had in her apron pocket."

Roy chuckled and said, "I do."

Virginia asked, "Oh no, Coy, what did you guys do?"

Roy said, "Hey, I didn't do anything this time. I was as pure as fresh snow. It was Coy who did it."

"Yeah, I confess. I came into the kitchen, walked up behind Mom and wrapped my arms around her. She thought I was just showing her some affection. She was just purring like a kitten, you know, her firstborn son being affectionate and all. I was actually slipping those worms into her pocket, the one where she had those little pieces of string. She had one of those worms tied into a square knot around a package before she realized what it was. Then I was running for my very life! In fact, that was the fastest old woman I had ever seen."

Virginia said, "I would have twisted your little punkin' head off your shoulders if it had been me."

"Yeah, you would have gone to sleep sometime," Maureen mused.

About that time, the Jinxs pulled up in their driveway. It was about 10:00 p.m. Jinx got out of his car and screamed as loud as he could, "Turn that radio down!"

Roy stood up, smiled and yelled back, "Sure, Jinxy, sure. No problem, Jinxy, old buddy, old pal."

As the evening wore on, the Bozemans noticed the lights go out in the Jinx's house. They waited for another hour before Roy went to the fence and picked up the string. He pulled it as tight as he could without breaking it. Coy held the rock resin in his hand. He winked at the others and started to rub the rock resin back and forth on the string with a few long strokes, some short strokes and a mixture of long short and jerky strokes. While the Bozemans were hiding behind the fence watching the Jinx's house, they could hear some of the most heart rendering and gosh awful sounds coming from the Jinx's house.

After about five minutes, there was a loud scream coming from inside the Jinx's home. The lights came on in an instant and the front door flew open. Mr. Jinx came running out like a frightened child and his wife and two sons came running out behind him. They all stood huddled together and appeared to be in a state of shock. Roy stood up and yelled over the fence, "I got ya, Jinxy! I got ya!" as he threw the string back over the fence.

Jinx, seeing the boys and their wives at the fence laughing at them, became furious and started screaming, "I'll get you, Roy! I'll get you for this. You hear me? I'll get you for this."

Roy said, "Sure, Jinxy. Here is the string, and the nail is in your house. I'm going to keep the secret ingredient for a keepsake."

Virginia said, "Come on y'all. Let's get a cup of tea before bed."

The four pranksters sat at the table having their tea. Virginia started to chuckle, and soon all four were laughing hysterically, as they were caught up in the moment. Between guffaws, Roy said, "I wish I had my camera out there. I would dearly love to have a picture of old Jinxy's face when he came running out of his house. I think he was so scared, he would have run off and left his family to fend for themselves."

Coy said, "You know, he would have. I have to admit, it was even more fun pulling off that prank tonight than it was when we did it to the neighbors in Bowden when we were kids."

"Yeah, you're right. I don't think those folks in Bowden were even half as scared as old Jinx was."

Maureen said to Virginia, "I think we were cheated while we grew up don't you? Can you imagine what it must have been like growing up with these two characters? The trouble is we would probably have all ended up in jail."

"Well, goodnight all," Coy said. "I think I'm going to call it quits for tonight. I'm all tuckered out."

Roy said, "Yep, me too."

The next morning, Maureen and Virginia were making breakfast when Coy and Roy came into the kitchen. Coy poured coffee for himself and Roy, who was saying, "Hey, Bubba, what do you say let's go out to fire lake and play some golf today?"

"That's a good idea. I could really use some leisure time."

After breakfast, the boys loaded up their golf clubs into Roy's truck and headed for the golf course. As the boys were teeing off on the third hole, Roy said to Coy, "Hey, Bubba, you have been awful quiet since we got here."

"I was just thinking, do you remember when you, me and the Bolus boys went out and caught all those birds, and then we turned them loose in the house?"

Roy started to laugh and he said, "Do I ever? Do you remember Dad running around through the house chasing those birds waving that old shotgun of his? It's a wonder he didn't end up blowing a hole in a wall or the ceiling."

"Yeah, well I was just wondering who we could pull that prank on."

Roy said, "How about our old friend Donny? After all, he would be about the most deserving person I could think of."

Coy chuckled and said, "He has caused the whole family some grief at one time or another."

The boys finished their game of golf. Roy shot his usual 78 and Coy shot his usual 121. The boys returned to the clubhouse and were about to order lunch when Maureen and Virginia came in to join them. After ordering lunch and some small talk, Roy asked Maureen and Virginia, "How would you two like to help us play a prank on someone very deserving?"

The two girls looked at each other, and Virginia asked, "Who would this person be and would we end up in jail?"

The boys laughed and said, "No, we won't end up in jail. The person would be some one who has at one time or another caused or created a situation in everyone's life. Donny."

Virginia said, "I was thinking I might want to try and stop you from playing your prank, but now I think we should hear all about this prank. Please don't spare the details."

Coy began to relate the story about the time Coy, Roy and the two Bolus boys had gone around to all the hay barns in the area where they lived and captured all the barn sparrows they could find. As they talked,

Maureen and Virginia were laughing. Virginia turned to Maureen and asked, "Why don't we go along with them?"

"Yes, I think we should. After all, we do have to keep an eye on them. Besides, it just may be sorta fun, too."

Later that evening after they had finished their dinner, Roy picked up the phone and called everyone he knew who owns a hay barn. Roy turned to the others and said, "They all said go for it. They hope we have a lot of fun and catch a lot of birds."

After gathering up all the boxes and containers they could find, the foursome loaded up and started out for their great adventure. While driving out into the country, Roy asked, "Virginia, did I ever tell you about the time Coy and I decided it was spring time and we should have a break in school to go fishing?"

"No, I don't think you did."

"Well," Roy said. "One afternoon after we got out of school, Coy and I were walking home and started talking about going fishing. One thing led to another, and we started to plan different ways to get out of school, short of getting really sick or dying. We got a great idea, but we figured we would need some help. We went over to visit with the Bolus boys. The four of us went out to the barn to discuss our idea. After all, you can't be to careful when your making the kind of plans we had in mind. The Bolus boy's parents had bought their sons two registered possum hounds. We had already gone out hunting with them and knew they would only hunt the very prey we had in mind."

"Bobby and Tommy were exited about our plan. Bobby said, 'We should be out of school for at least a week.' And so the scheme was set to go."

Roy continued, "That evening, we gathered up everything we could find to hold our prey. We figured since the Pretty Water school house was only a two room school, we would probably only need ten or fifteen of these little guys to do the job."

"In less than ten minutes, those dogs had found and helped us capture five of them. We hurried over and released them under the school. We even threw in a few dinner scraps and were off to find more of these wonder working little fellows."

"It took us about three hours to get the rest of them. We put them under the school with their friends, blocked the entrance hole and headed for home. On the way home, it occurred to us we had better go to the creek and take a serious bath. We bathed in that cold creek water for at least a half hour. We thought we smelled pretty good."

"When Coy and I walked into the house and climbed into bed, we heard Dad yell, 'Whoa! Did you boys bring home a skunk?' We answered, 'No sir, we didn't.' He responded, 'Then go outside and run that thing off.' We said, 'Yes, sir.'"

"We went outside laughing, trying hard not to be heard. We came back a few minutes later and Dad asked if we saw anything. We of course answered yes, and told him there were two of them. He said, 'To bad you couldn't have run off that smell as well.'"

"The next morning we got up early and went to school. We met the Bolus boys and laughed all the way to school. We stayed close to the building so that no one could tell if it was us or the school that smelled so bad. I'm sure there were those who had their opinion."

"When the teachers arrived and opened the classrooms, they were already complaining about the smell. Not wanting to arouse suspicion, we complained to. After entering the classrooms, the odor was so strong that some of the kids were getting sick, some were crying and it looked as if Mr. Stoat was about to become violently ill. The teachers ran everyone out of the classrooms and sent everyone home. They said it would take at least a week to air the school out. All the way home we were laughing and singing. We had a whole week to go fishing!"

"About a week later, a school board member named Mr. James came by our house. He asked our Dad if he thought Coy and I might possibly know anything about how those pesky little skunks got under the school house. Mr. James brought out their lunch of what appeared to be some left over fried chicken and gravy with a few biscuits."

"After Mr. James left, Dad called us in and sat us down and said, 'I know you did it. I can't prove it, but I know you did it. It is amazing. We had fried chicken with gravy, and biscuits for dinner the other night. That would be the same night that I smelled a skunk right after you two came into this house. I could not tell that man for sure, but you sure as hell had better not do anything like this again. I don't care how much you like to fish. You know I just can't wait until you have kids of your own. I sincerely hope they're just as rotten as you are.'"

Maureen and Virginia were laughing so hard, tears were streaming down their cheeks. Roy said, "Well party people, our first barn is coming up just over the hill."

After arriving at the first barn, Coy said to the girls, "This is what we want you two to do. You shine your light up on one of the rafters near the wall. Then slowly swing the light beam along the rafter toward the center of the barn. When you have a bird in the center of the light beam, just hold the light steady while Roy and I shimmy out on the rafter and catch the bird. We do that same thing until we catch enough birds."

The girls dutifully held the lights, while Coy and Roy caught the birds and lowered them down to the girls. The girls would then place the birds in the larger boxes. After about a dozen barns, Coy and Roy decided they had enough birds for the prank. Besides, after both boys had fallen off the rafters several times, even landing on bales of hay can start to feel bad. So the midnight cowboys and girls were headed to their old buddy, Donny's house.

It was about midnight when our pranksters arrived at Donny's house. After unloading all the boxes of birds, they parked the truck across the street in the shadow of a large tree. The first thing they had to do was find a window that was not locked. It didn't take very long before they found a bedroom window at the back of the house. It was not only unlocked, but standing wide open. The boys released the birds into the house and closed the window. They ran back to the truck where the girls were waiting.

After putting the boxes in the truck, the lights started to come on in Donny's bedroom. When he opened the door, a very large black cloud came into his room. Even across the street, the pranksters could hear things such as lamps and knick-knacks being knocked over as the birds were flying around the room. It was only a few minutes until the front door flew open, and out came the huge black cloud with Donny right behind it screaming at the top of his lungs. As all the lights on his block started to come on, Donny suddenly realized his nudity and ran back into the house, slamming the door behind him.

Roy said, "You know he will never, ever figure out how those birds got into his house."

Coy said, "Yep! And we ain't never, ever gonna tell him either, are we?"

When the pranksters got home and sat down to have breakfast, they were still laughing and reliving their all night prank. Maureen said to Virginia, "If we go to jail today it was worth it, don't you think?"

Chapter 6

Later that evening, the boys were sitting on the patio talking about their childhood. "Roy," Coy asked. "Do you remember that old 1940 Ford hood boat we found when we were kids?"

"Yes, I do. You almost drowned me with that old boat."

Coy said, "Yeah, but you have to admit we sure had a whole lot of fun with it."

"Yep. Don't ya kinda wish we still had it?"

Coy agreed, "It would be kinda fun to take our girls for a midnight boat ride, don't you think?"

Roy kinda giggled and said, "Well, where do we get parts and when do we take those fine looking gals on this midnight dinner cruise?"

"We ain't doing nothing right now, so why don't we go around to some of the junkyards and see what we can find."

And with that the two old kids at heart left the house in search of adventure. At the third junk yard they found what they were looking for with a bonus. They found two old 1940 ford hoods and two old 1940 Chevy hoods. Coy said, "Hey, Bubba, let's get those Chevy hoods too. We can build two canoes and have us a ford and a Chevy race."

Roy said, "Yeah, but we better make up two of those grappling hook and rope setups. Is this going to be boys against girls, or will it be me and Virginia against you and Maureen?"

"We better think about that for awhile."

The boys took their old car hoods to a welding shop. Since they expected the boats might sink, they decided to have them painted a bright yellow and a bright red. That night at dinner, Coy and Roy started talking about the fun times they had with an old boat they had when they were kids. Maureen and Virginia were all ears. Roy said, "I know where we can get a couple of boats, and Virginia and Maureen can make us a nice picnic dinner. Would y'all like to go on a moon light canoe ride?"

Virginia looked at Maureen and asked, "What do you think?"

Maureen answered, "Well, that bird thingy was a lot of fun. Let's do it."

The next day was kind of uneventful. Maureen and Virginia went to the beauty shop and had their hair done for the moonlight canoe ride. Coy and Roy spent the day playing golf and laughing about the coming events.

The next evening the boys loaded up their car hood canoes and the girls loaded up the picnic dinner. Virginia kept looking at the boats with more than a little skepticism. Finally, she asked the boys, "Are you guys sure these things you call canoes are going to float?"

Coy replied, "Oh yeah, we had one just like these when we were kids. In fact, we are going to float down the same creek that we did when we were kids."

Maureen looked at Virginia and said, "Somehow that doesn't sound to reassuring."

When they arrived at the creek, Coy and Roy unloaded the boats and put them in the water. The two girls looked at each other and Virginia said, "I am amazed. I had my doubts. I didn't think those things would float."

The girls started to unload the picnic baskets when Coy said, "Maureen, this little beach area here is a really nice little spot to have our dinner. So why not just leave the dinner in the truck? We will go down the creek and when we get back, we can build a little fire and have our dinner here."

Maureen and Virginia both agreed. With that, the boys started getting the boats ready to go. Coy went to the truck and got the two grappling hook and rope devices. Virginia asked, "Hey, what are those things and what are they for?"

Roy said, "They're just safety devices. We probably won't need them at all."

They all started to get into the boats. For about fifteen minutes, they were all rolling out of the boats into the water. The two boys were laughing hysterically, but the girls didn't see the humor at all. At one point, the girls suggested that the boys were deliberately causing them to fall into the water.

The boys dutifully held the red boat steady and let the girls get in and get set. Roy said, "Why don't you girls go ahead and start down stream. We will be right behind you."

With that Maureen and Virginia started to paddle down stream. Coy and Roy got into the yellow boat and started to follow. They only got a couple of hundred yards when they saw the girls go for a swim, as their boat went to the bottom. So the boys paddled to the shore, and using one of the grappling hooks, pulled the boat to shore. They held the boat for the girls and helped them to get going again.

After watching the girls swim ashore and retrieving the boat four times, and having the girls call them some very unfriendly names, Maureen and Virginia finally started to get the hang of handling this odd boat.

The four went down the creek for about a mile. Things had been going pretty well, so Maureen suggested that she get in the boat with Coy, and Virginia get in with Roy. The boys didn't know the girls had a little surprise of their own. Right on cue, both Maureen and Virginia jumped over the front of the boats. They laughed with glee as the two boats stood straight up on end and sank out of sight, carrying the two boys down with them. After swimming ashore they all had a good laugh. They retrieved the boats using the grappling hooks and finished their boat ride back to the little beach.

While they ate their dinner, Coy told the girls about a time when they were kids. One winter after a flood, Coy and Roy were going down the creek in their old canoe, when they found a boat about twelve feet long sunk close to the creek bank. They tried to pull it up on the bank, but couldn't move it. They managed to get it up over the roots of a tree that grew out of the bank, but still could not get the back of the boat over to the bank.

Coy talked Roy into taking the canoe and getting the front of the canoe under the back of the boat and paddling to push the back of the boat over to the bank. Well it seemed like a good idea at the time, but it was winter and very cold. The canoe slipped out from under the boat and stood on end. It slowly sank carrying Roy down with it.

Coy was laughing so hard he could hardly tell the story. He said he wished he could have had a picture of the look on Roy's face. Roy, however, thought his big brother had taken advantage of his kindness and meek manner, not only in the canoe incidence, but in most of the others as well. Virginia said, "Oh my, Roy, you may be a kind person, but meek? In your dreams!"

Roy blushed and they all started to laugh. Roy said, "Virginia, just down the road about a mile is where me and Coy worked at that old dairy. I don't think I ever told you about the time we decided to go rabbit hunting. Me and Coy got together with the Bolus boys and a couple of other guys. I don't think we even realized the next morning was Monday morning. Anyway, we all met at the dairy and brought our 22 rifles. After work, we picked up our rifles and walked out of the barn. There was a strange car driving up to the barn. We had no idea who it was, but I guess the guy saw all of us with those rifles and must have panicked. He seemed like he was in a hurry. When he tried to turn around, he ran into a tree and a fence. He finally left without speaking to us at all."

"A day or two later, the sheriff came out to visit with our Dad. I am sure he went to the other boy's Dads as well. It seems that fella was the truant officer. He told everyone we were an out of control teenage gang and that he had enough trouble in his life. He didn't need to go way out in the country to be threatened by a gang of moon shiners kids packing guns."

"Dad called us in right in front of the sheriff and asked us about the incident. At first we didn't have a clue what they were talking about. Once they told us what day and where it happened, then it became clear. We then told them what had actually happened."

"After Dad and the sheriff had a good laugh, the sheriff said he was sorry the man quit his job, but it was probably for the best. He did say that we had better not do anything like that again."

After just kicking back, watching the stars, and listening to the Coyotes off in the distance, the boys and their lovely young ladies decided it was time to go home. They put out the fire and started for home.

Maureen and Virginia were hoping Coy and Roy weren't going to dream up another prank. Unfortunately, both boys were already dreaming of something else to do.

The next morning, Coy and Roy were still sleeping, when the most tantalizing aroma of bacon, eggs and fresh coffee drifted into the bedrooms. Both boys jumped out of bed, dressed quickly and rushed into the dining room where Maureen and Virginia were sitting. As everyone started to eat, Roy said, "Oh, I really wish we had us some fresh milk. There ain't nothing like good old fresh cows milk for breakfast."

Virginia said, "I am so sorry, Baby. First of all, we don't have a cow. Secondly, I thought cooking your breakfast was enough, without having to go out and milk a cow too. How about you Maureen? What do you think?"

"Well, I have milked a cow before," Maureen answered. "I think store bought milk is just fine. You two can settle for the store bought, or go milk your own cow, ok?"

Coy and Roy looked at each other with a smirk. It seems Maureen and Virginia had come up with a great idea. It seems the two pranksters would have to find themselves a milk cow. Right after breakfast, the two old boys climbed into Roy's pickup truck and headed out into the country looking for a dairy. All Roy could talk about was how good breakfast would be in the morning with fresh milk.

After driving around in the country sipping coffee from a thermos and talking about the good old days, their eyes came across a great big beautiful dairy. It looked like there were at least a hundred milk cows. Roy said, "Bubba, my mouth is a watering already. How are we going to get my milk and get it home for in the morning?"

Coy said, "Well, the first thing we have to do is go into town and get us a rope and a milk bucket. Then we have to wait until it gets dark to go milk a cow. Are you up to it Bubba?"

On the way back to town Coy said, "You know, Bubba, it might be a lot easier to just go up to the farmer and buy the milk in the first place."

"True, but it wouldn't be as much fun would it?"

"No," Coy agreed. "You are sure right there."

So when they got back to town, Coy and Roy headed to the grange country store to buy a rope and a milk bucket. The boys went back home and spent the rest of the day watching a little TV and napping.

After dinner, Roy announced that he and Coy were going to go to the bowling alley to watch some of the local bowlers, and would be back in a couple of hours. The boys headed out for their fresh milk adventure. Coy said, "Roy, do you remember when we would take the hounds down on the creek at night in the summer when we were kids? We would build up a fire and the Bolus boys would come down with their dogs. We would get our old carbide lamps fired up, make a pot of coffee and then turn the dogs loose and listen to them run through the trees, trying to find the scent of an old raccoon."

Roy said, "Yeah, I can almost hear them start to bay as they pick up the scent."

"Kids today will probably never experience the thrill of a coon hunt. We sit by the fire, listening to the dogs looking for a scent. Then when the scent gets a little warmer, the dogs yelp and bawl as they actually see the raccoon and give chase."

"Oh yeah," Roy remembered. "The dogs would jump up and go running, and we would chase them as fast as we could. We ran through the trees and under brush, trying to catch up to the dogs. We would trip over roots and logs and fall on our faces. Then we would hear the dogs start to get exited and kind of yodel when they have a coon up a tree."

"Kids today wouldn't want to do those kinds of things though." Coy continued, "Hey, remember when the dogs treed in a hole under a creek bank? Bobby was showing us how brave he was and reached in to grab that old coon by his back legs."

Roy started to bust up, "Boy was he surprised when he pulled that old bob cat out instead. Talk about having a tiger by the tail and not being able to turn it loose."

"I thought he was going to pass out spinning around like that to keep that cat from getting a hold of him. You know, lucky for us though, it was going away from all of us when it slipped out of his hands. That could have been nasty for us."

Roy laughing said, "Yeah, you're right. It must have taken Bobby fifteen minutes to get his head straight. He was so dizzy he almost passed out."

Coy said, "I think that old cat was pretty dizzy too. He sort of ran funny when he took off."

"Hey, Bubba, there is our pasture coming up."

As they pulled up to the cow pasture, Roy pulled the pick up over to the side of the road and turned off the engine. It was pretty dark by this time. Coy and Roy climbed out of the truck, took their rope and bucket, and headed out into the pasture to find a milk cow.

As they were looking for a cow, neither of them gave a thought to the fact that these cows had never been milked out in the pasture or at dark. Most animals are afraid of being held against their will in the dark. With nothing but fresh milk on their minds, the boys continued on their quest for milk.

Just then, Coy spotted a really big Holstein cow. "Oh Bubba," Coy called out softly. "I hope your bucket is big enough, cause this one looks like she is going to give us about five gallons of milk."

Roy said, "You rope and hold her, I will do the milking."

With that, Coy roped the cow. She promptly started to jump and buck. Coy was doing a pretty good job of holding her, until he stepped in a very large pile of very fresh cow manure. His feet flew out from under him, allowing him to drop flat on his back into the fresh manure. The cow dragged him all the way through it, smearing him from his hip pockets to the back of his head. Roy grabbed on to the rope and helped to get the cow under control. Coy looped the rope around the cow's left front leg. Coy said, "I sure hope all her bellowing didn't wake up the whole world."

"Me too," Roy said as he was trying to talk between guffaws. "We better hurry up, get our milk and get out of here. It sure was great getting to see the funny part for a change."

Coy said, "Well you better hurry up and get that milk so we can get out of here."

Roy went to run around behind her, not realizing the cow had developed a case of diarrhea from her scare. Roy slipped in the manure, falling into it on his back. The cow kicked the bucket out of Roy's hand. He hurried and grabbed the bucket to get it under the cow to milk. She flipped her tail, which was full of fresh manure, all the way around Roy's head. When she pulled it back, she left a green stripe covering his face and head.

Roy got the bucket back under the cow and started to milk as fast as he could. In the meantime, Coy was looking up at the stars trying not to laugh hysterically. The two boys were so intent on getting their milk, neither of them saw the two men walking up behind them. They almost jumped out of their skin when they heard a voice say, "Boys, I am Sheriff Bohan, and this here is Jim Johnson, the man that owns that cow you have your rope on. Now to tell the truth, we were just trying to figure out what exactly y'all are doing. For instance, are you trying to steal the cow, or are you trying to steal the milk? Or perhaps, are you trying to steal some cow manure? Do you suppose maybe you could enlighten us on this subject?

With his head down, Coy sheepishly said, "My baby brother over there wanted some fresh cow milk for breakfast. To tell the truth we thought it would be fun to get the milk straight from the cow ourselves. Obviously we were wrong. Mr. Johnson we hope you will accept our sincere apology."

"Sheriff," Roy said. "Do you think before you take us to jail, we could go by our house and take a shower and change clothes?"

Jim Johnson said, "Sheriff, I think these old boys have learned a lesson. In fact, I don't know when I have had such a good laugh in years. I think we can just let them go, after I get them a jar of fresh cow's milk and they promise from now on they will come to my house in the day time to get their milk. So what do you think sheriff?"

"Well, it's ok with me. I must admit this has been about the funniest call I have ever been on. Oh, by the way you two, it is against the law to drive down the road naked in this state. At least keep your underwear on and don't try this again. Jim, I'll be seeing you."

Mr. Johnson said, "Well fellows, there is a water trough over there by that tree. Why don't you go over there and clean up some and I will be right back."

The boys were just about cleaned up in about twenty minutes, when Mr. Johnson returned and handed them some coveralls. He said, "I found these old coveralls in the barn. You might as well wear them home and here is a jar of fresh milk. I hope you boys will come back and see us again sometime, in the day time of course."

The red faced old boys said, "Yes sir. You can count on it."

On the way home, Coy said, "You know, Bubba, he was a mighty nice fella back there. In fact, it was kinda like that old time Oklahoma hospitality."

"Yeah," Roy agreed. "He could have thrown the book at us."

When Coy and Roy got home, they took their smelly clothes into the garage and went into the house through the back door. Maureen and Virginia were in the kitchen fixing a snack. When the boys came in, Maureen and Virginia looked at each other and at exactly the same time asked, "What is that smell?"

Maureen said, "If I didn't know better, I would think a cow just came into the kitchen."

Roy sat the milk on the counter. Virginia looked at the milk, then at the two troublesome 60+ teenagers, and asked, "How in the world could you two go to the bowling alley, get a gallon of milk, change your clothes from some nice jeans and shirts to some worn out coveralls, and smell like you have been rolling in cow poop for a week? Further more how do you expect us to believe it?"

Roy said, "Honey we…"

Virginia said, "Don't talk to me right now. I don't want to hear it."

Maureen said, "Both of you go out, put your clothes in to wash and then take a bath. Please use some soap and shampoo. When you are done, then you will tell us the truth about what you did, or else."

Both Coy and Roy left the room and headed to the bathrooms. While the boys were in taking a shower, Maureen and Virginia sat down at the table to have their coffee. Virginia said, "I just can't wait to hear this one."

Maureen agreed, "I can't either, but I sure wish we could have seen what that sheriff and farmer saw."

"Yeah, in fact, I'll bet their still laughing about it."

Maureen said, "I sure hope if they see our husbands that we aren't with them. It would be embarrassing if they started to go 'Moo! Moo!' toward the guys."

When Coy and Roy came back into the room, Virginia sat a glass of their ill-gotten milk in front of each of them. Maureen started, "We thought you might like to wash down your crow with some of your fresh milk."

Both Maureen and Virginia burst out laughing so hard, they had tears streaming down their faces. Coy said, "Come on, Bubba, let's go out on the patio and have a cup of coffee. We don't have to have our kind, loving wives destroy what's left of our dignity."

"Yeah, come on, Bubba."

Virginia backpedaled, "Wait, Roy, and you to, Coy. We didn't mean any harm. We were just having some fun too."

Coy looked back at the two girls and said, "Sure, we understand. We wouldn't want to embarrass you would we. Bubba?"

Roy said, "No, we sure wouldn't. I mean you never know when someone could be overheard saying things like, 'Moo! Moo!' Let's go, Bubba."

After the boys left the room, Virginia said Maureen, "I really didn't mean to hurt their feelings."

"Neither did I, but I guess we really did it this time."

Coy closed the patio door behind himself and his brother. Both of the brothers looked at each other and started to bust up with laughter. Maureen started to open the door to the patio about the same time Coy and Roy started to laugh. She turned to Virginia and said, "Their feelings aren't hurt. In fact, they are out there laughing their fool heads off at us."

Virginia said, "Why those turds! Let's go give them their milk."

So the girls picked up the glasses of milk, promptly walked out on the patio and threw the milk into the brother's faces. They went back into the house and burst into laughter. Roy looked at Coy and said, "I think they heard us laughing at them, don't you?"

"I reckon they did. You know, Bubba, all this talk about cow poop though has given me an idea. You know how that old man out in Pretty Water keeps getting it over on us?"

Roy said, "Yeah, so what are you thinking?"

"Well, we haven't seen him in years and he seems awfully spry to be as old as he is. I was just thinking, I would like to see him for real, you know, to see what good shape he is in. Wouldn't you?"

"Well yeah," Roy agreed. "But, I don't want to get shot in the process of seeing his face."

"Hey, I don't either. But I think I have an idea. Let me think about it for a while and I'll tell you in the morning."

Chapter 7

The boys were sitting on the patio the next morning when Coy said, "You know, Bubba, I was just thinking about last night. All the talk about cow poop and all I got me an idea on how we can get that old man to come out, so we can see his face."

Roy said, "Bubba, that old man doesn't have any cows."

"I know that."

Roy asked, "So are we going to milk one of his horses?"

"No we are not going to milk his horses. Just wait until tonight and I will show you, ok?"

"Ok," Roy agreed.

Later that evening, the boys told Maureen and Virginia a large fib about going out to visit a friend, and headed for the Pretty Water area. On the way, they stopped at a farm and picked up some cow exhaust to use. When they got to the old mans house, Roy asked, "Coy, what are we going to do with this stuff?"

"Just be patient. You'll see when we get there."

It was dark out when they arrived at the old man's farm. After parking the truck down the road, they put the soft gooey cow exhaust in a double paper bag. The boys walked up the road to the old mans house. Coy handed Roy some matches and said, "Here Roy. Go up to the door, sit the bag down and light it on fire. Knock loudly on the door and run as fast as you can back out here in the dark, ok?"

"Hey," Roy complained. "Why does it have to be me that goes up to the door?"

"Well, like you're always telling me, you are the youngest so you should be the fastest, right?"

After thinking for a few moments, Roy said, "Well I guess so," and headed for the front door. As soon as he reached the door, he sat the bag down and set fire to it. He ran as fast as his tired old legs would carry him back out on the road. Roy had just reached the safety of the darkness when the old man opened the door. Seeing the fire, he started to stamp the fire out with both feet splattering the very fresh cow poop all over himself.

The old man came out to use the outside faucet to clean himself up. He was screaming a lot of dirty words and things like "I'm gonna kill you when I find out who you are! Mark my words, you, you demons!"

Coy and Roy looked at each other in amazement, "Hey, He's just a kid," Coy said. "You know, I'll bet he must be that old man's grandson."

"Well, he must have spent a lotta time with his grandpa, cause he knew all the old pranks."

Coy said, "Yeah, but we finally got one over on him by playing a new one."

On the way home, both Coy and Roy kept laughing and reliving the moment. They stopped at a grocery store on the way and bought an apple pie and ice cream to celebrate their hard earned victory when they got home.

They came into the house still laughing hysterically. Maureen and Virginia were in the living room, and came running into the kitchen to see what was wrong. They stopped short, as soon as they saw the two old men. Virginia asked, "What happened? You both look like you have just come from church or a movie. You don't look like you have been out to the Pretty Water area getting into trouble. You're so clean. What happened? Did you finally grow up?"

Coy and Roy started to laugh. Roy grabbed Virginia and started to waltz her around the dining room, as the boys told the girls in unison, "We did go out to the old mans farm and this time we got one over on him."

Roy told the girls all about the prank they had played on the old man. He told how he was the hero this time, lighting the bag on fire and running away before getting caught. Then he said, "Virginia, we saw that old man tonight and it is no wonder he kept catching us. He is just a wet nosed kid. He must be the old mans grandson. He has to be in his late 20's or early 30's."

Maureen asked, "Does this mean you're going to stop going out there and pestering that poor man?"

The boys looked at each other, and Coy said, "Yeah, I guess so. It ain't no fun anymore now." Coy asked, "Maureen, honey, did I ever tell you about the time I had to much to drink and I didn't get into trouble for it?"

Maureen said, "No you haven't."

"When we lived in Cleveland," Coy continued, "there was this old black man that lived on a farm back behind our farm. He would come over, ever so often, to trade with my Dad. On one occasion, he brought over some freshly cleaned rabbits with a recipe for barbeque rabbit. Mom cooked them up, but she must have done something wrong. They were so bad, when Mom threw them out for the barn cats, the cats buried them."

"Anyway, the old man came over one hot summer afternoon. He was wearing a carpenter's apron. In the pockets, he had some ice and some bottles of his home made beer. He offered my Dad and Uncle Calvin some samples. We were all squatted down on our heels. I was squatted down between my Dad and uncle. Like I said, it was hot, so Dad would give me a sip of his beer, and my uncle would give me a sip of his beer. Neither of them knew the other was giving it to me. Since I was only seven years old, it didn't take very much to get me in a funny state of mind."

"My mother came out of the house to tell my Dad that we had to get ready to go to my grandmother's house. She saw me standing beside the car counting chickens. She observed one old banty hen running back and forth under the car. Mom said, 'Dale, I hope you have a really good story to tell your mother.' Dad asked, 'Why?' Mom said, 'Look at your son. He is drunker than a Sailor.'"

The next morning the two old guys came out to have some breakfast. When they came into the dining room, Maureen and Virginia were sitting at the table, reading the front page of the newspaper. When they realized that Coy and Roy were in the room, they put the paper down flat on the table and asked, "Would you two like to read the front page of the paper?"

Coy said, "No, actually I think we would rather have some bacon and eggs."

"You know, I think some blueberry pancakes would be good too," Roy added.

Virginia said, "Coy and Roy, that wasn't a question. Read the paper."

"Well if you are going to put it that way, ok."

The boys looked at the paper, then at each other. The headline read, "Pranksters have been harassing a Pretty Water farmer, Mr. Clonnas. Mr. Clonnas says he remembers there were two boys who harassed his grandfather the same way when he was a child. 'In fact,' he said. 'They played the very same pranks on grandpa, like stealing his water melons, riding his horses in his pasture and sliding down his hay stacks. I would almost think it was the same guys, but it can't be. They would be in their late sixties or maybe in their early seventies. Maybe they have grandchildren with the same sick sense of humor.' Mr. Connas says he is going to go back through his grandpa's things to see if he can find a name. He said he would really like to a get good nights sleep for a change. If anyone knows who might be playing these pranks, please contact the newspaper or at least ask them to please stop."

Coy looked over at Roy and said, "Hey, we don't have any more pranks for him anyway. We thought we were still playing with the old man, so he can rest easy, at least for a while. Right, Bubba?"

"Yeah, I need a rest too and I think our bodies could use some time to heal up."

Maureen jumped in, "Oh no! You are going to leave this guy alone period. If he finds your name in his grandfather's things, it won't be hard to find you. There are not that many Bozemans in Oklahoma. Now you got it?"

Both boys nodded and asked, "Do you suppose we could have those eggs, bacon and pancakes now please? We are awfully hungry."

Things were pretty quiet for a month or so. Coy and Roy decided to show the girls some of the sights around the great state of Oklahoma. There was the Indian village in Ardmore, Oklahoma. The girls were able to see the different types of dwellings that the different tribes lived in. They learned about the people and some of their customs.

There were the zoos in both Oklahoma City and Tulsa. The boys took the girls to see some of the places where they had lived, and showed them a lake that wasn't there when they grew up. In fact, they had lived in a town that is now under the lake. There were golf games, barbeques on the patio and lots of quite times. However, Maureen and Virginia had an uneasy feeling deep down in side, wondering when these two old kids at heart would go on another adventure.

One Saturday evening, Roy and Virginia's grandchildren were over and the boys were cooking dinner on the patio. Remembering the good old days, Coy said, "Roy, do you remember when Mom and Dad were gone all night, and we decided to keep that old man up for a while?"

"Yeah, but I don't think these kids have heard this one."

"Well," Coy continued. "Like I said, Mom and Dad were gone and it was a really bright moonlit night. Roy and I could see the old man's water tank as plain as day. It sat up on top of this old iron tower. We knew there was no water in it so we decided to shoot at it with our 22 rifles. We opened the front room window and waited for the old man to go to bed."

"It was probably about nine or ten when his lights went out. Roy and I aimed our rifles at the tank and let go. It seemed like twenty minutes went by, but it was only a few seconds, when we heard the sound of those bullets hitting that old tank. There was a loud, 'Dong, dong!'"

"Those lights came back on and his dogs were running around going nuts. That old fellow came ripping out of his house in his long johns, waving that shot gun of his. After about ten minutes, his dogs went back to the porch and lay back down, and the old man went back in the house. We watched the windows of his house, and in a few minutes, the lights went back off. We waited about twenty minutes to give him time to go back to sleep. Then we took aim on the old tank again and let fire. 'Dong, dong!'"

As before, those dogs went crazy and the old man was back outside in his underwear. We played this game with the old fella 'til around 1:00 a.m. It was sure a lot of fun messing with that old guy. I sure miss those days."

Roy said, "You know, Coy and I worked at a dairy for a while. We had to use these old large milking machines that you strap over the cows back and fastened. That way, it wouldn't fall off. The milking machine hung under the cow's udder."

"Well, we thought we would like to see how fast the machine would milk the cow. We turned the machine up as fast as it would go, and then, we got busy doing something else. All of a sudden, we heard this loud sucking noise. Before we could get to that old cow, she had ripped out the stanchion and was running out the door with the milking machine still hanging under her. We ran as fast as we could go, trying to catch her, but she was really taking off. I guess the clanging of her legs as she was kicking that old machine, must have scared her half to death."

"It really beat up that old milking machine too. We thought we were going to have to buy it for a while there, and we were really scared, because we didn't think we were ever going to catch her. The machine finally fell of and she settled down, but she was sure hard to get in the milk barn after that."

Roy's daughter Tina asked, "How long did you two work at the dairy?"

Roy answered, "Just a few months."

Tina asked, "Was that the only thing that you two did while you worked there?"

"No," Coy said. "The owner, Mr. Philips, milked two breeds of cows. He milked Holstein cows, because they gave him a large volume of milk. He also milked brown Swiss cows, because they gave him the butterfat to make the milk richer."

"Mr. Philips bought a yearling bull calf from another farmer and had him delivered to the dairy. He was a friendly calf and we sort of liked playing with him. We would go up to him and push against his head and he would push back. This went on every day until he got to big for us to play this game with him. One morning, we were cleaning the lot around the barn with an old john deer tractor. The bull was just standing there watching. I sort of, by accident of course, drove the tractor up to him. He accidentally put his head against the front of the tractor. I guess I sort of pushed against him a little, and he pushed back. So we started a new game and we played this game for a couple of months or so."

"Well, that bull got to be about 2000 pounds. He was full-grown now, so he was put out in the main pasture with the cows. Mr. Philips came out to the dairy one morning but didn't stop at the barn. He drove his brand new Ford pickup right out in the pasture. We just stood there petrified with fear. You know how you just know something bad is going to happen and you're going to die because of it? In a few minutes, Mr. Philips came walking back up to the barn, swearing like a sailor. He said, 'If I had a gun, I would shoot that crazy bull!'"

"As if we didn't know, we asked him, 'What happened?'"

"He said, 'That crazy bull! That was a brand new pickup I only bought one hour ago. I drove it straight out here from the car lot. That stupid bull! I was just driving along through the pasture, about one mile an hour, and that bull walked up to the front of my brand new pickup. I honked my horn at him, but he just kept on coming. So, I just blared the horn and tried to stop. He just put his head right in the center of my new pickup's grill and pushed in the whole front end into the engine fan. He even caved in the front bumper. When I got out of the pickup, he was still pushing it backwards, so I ran for my life.'"

"'I got to the fence and looked back. He had left the truck, and was moseying out into the pasture. You know, maybe bulls really don't like the color red. Maybe I better get a blue truck.'"

"I guess we got lucky he didn't kill the bull or us!"

Roy was just starting to turn the steaks on the grill when the back door flew open and his granddaughter, Diana, came running out screaming at Roy's great grandson Cameron. Cameron had just shot the dog with his BB gun. She grabbed the gun out of his hands and said, "You are not going to get this back ever!"

Roy asked her, "What did he do?"

She told him, "He shot your dog."

Roy said, "Well, I got to tell you, me and Bubba over there didn't shoot any dogs. I seem to remember when we hid behind some trees and shot Dad's old bull, in that part that hung down back there between his back legs. I tell you, when that BB hit, that old bull would let out a beller and jump straight up in the air. All four legs would go in different directions, and he would spin around like a helicopter. He had a look of murder in his eyes. I think if he had seen us he would have run through hell fire, walls, trees or anything to get to us. I mean he was really mad."

"Yeah," Coy said. "I seem to remember an incident with a bicycle and a BB gun on a gravel road coming down a hill. Right, Bubba?"

"Yeah, I do. I bet your going to tell it too, aren't you?"

"Yep," Coy replied. "We lived up in Mannford, and one afternoon, Roy got on my bicycle and pushed it up the hill, and came just a ripping down the hill. After he had come down the hill a few times, I yelled at him to let me have a turn. Well, he just laughed and kept on having himself a good time. So I went into the house and got my BB gun. I went out onto the road and waved it at him and said, 'If you don't give me a turn on my bike, I am going to shoot you off of it.'"

"Roy just laughed at me as he went by, yelling out, 'You don't have any BBs.'"

"So I squatted down there in the road and picked up almost a hand full of little tiny rocks. As Roy was coming down the hill again laughing, he yelled, 'You don't have any BBs!'"

"By the way, he didn't have a shirt on. I cocked that BB gun, aimed and fired. I got him right in the back! He threw up his arms and flopped in the middle of the road. I thought it was pretty funny, until I realized Dad would be coming home soon. I was probably going to pay for my indiscretion with my life."

"Yeah," Roy remembered. "If my memory serves me correctly, we were playing out in the road when Dad came home. He was driving that old farm tractor. As he went by, you ran up from behind the tractor, grabbed the fender and jumped up on the tow bar. Dad just kept going. But when I came running up and grabbed the fender, he slammed on the brakes before I could jump up. I ran into that iron tow bar with both shins. In fact, I was probably still running about ninety miles an hour. I do believe you, my loving brother, and my loving and protective father, were both laughing your fool heads off. I was lying in the middle of the road, crying my poor little eyes out, in pain and agony. In fact, I can still feel it today every time I think about it. It grieves me, and I just want to go sit in a corner and tickle my own feet."

Virginia asked, "Roy, why on earth would you want to do that? Wouldn't that be kind of silly?"

Roy's face turned red and he said, "I didn't mean it that way. I was trying to make a point."

By this time they were all laughing in hysterics. Coy said, "Bubba, I think those steaks are done, don't you?"

"Yeah,' Roy answered. "Virginia, why don't we set this table out here and bring out the wine, salad and the rest of the dinner?"

"Ok. I'll tell Diana to bring the boys out and fix their plates."

Maureen asked, "What do you want me to do?"

Virginia replied, "Just sit down and fix your plate."

After dinner they were all sitting on the patio, enjoying coffee and talking about the good old days. As Roy was looking up at the stars, he said, "You know, the stars don't seem as bright as they did when we were kids, do they?"

Maureen said, "Well, they never seemed that bright in the city where I grew up."

"I remember," Virginia said, "When we were kids, the stars were so bright you could see around the area. Heck, you could walk out to the fence and see the cows in the pasture. The lightning bugs were like little, tiny, white Christmas lights."

"Yeah," Coy remembered. "Maybe God saw all the bad things people were doing and dimmed the lights so He couldn't see so much."

Roy agreed, "Maybe you're right, but do you think maybe He knows we were just boys trying to have fun?"

"Bubba, I wasn't talking about us when we were kids. I meant the things people are doin' all over the world that just ain't right. Know what I mean?" Coy asked. "Roy, is that old house out in Pretty Water still standing? You know every time we have gone out there, it's been dark. We haven't actually gone by the house."

"You know, I really don't know I haven't gone by it either. Why don't we go out there and have a look see in the morning?"

"Ok," Coy agreed. "Maureen, do you and Virginia want to go with us?"

Virginia said, "No, we have some shopping to do."

"Well, it's late and I think it's time for me to take these boys home and put them to bed." Diana said. "I will say goodnight, and thanks for dinner. Boys, give hugs and kisses."

After Diana left, Maureen said, "I think it's bedtime."

Everyone said goodnight and went off to their bedrooms for a good nights rest.

Chapter 8

The next morning after a big breakfast, the two old men climbed into Roy's truck and headed for the Pretty Water area again. Maureen and Virginia took Virginia's car and headed for the mall. As they were driving down the road, Coy asked, "Roy, do you remember that old red '49 Ford I had? You know the one that grew grass in the back floorboard every time it rained?"

Roy said, "Oh yeah. Do you remember the time you painted the spotlight bulbs red with Barbara's finger nail polish?"

"Yeah, I thought that would be so much fun and it was for a while."

"Yep," Roy remembered. "Hooking the turn signal blinker up to the spotlights was clever to. Remember those very embarrassed young people when we pulled into those lovers' lanes?"

Coy said, "It was a good thing we picked the lovers' lanes in the Keystone area. If we had done that around home, we would have been in big, big trouble. Everyone knew that old Ford of mine."

"Well, here we are and there is the old pond," Roy said. "Remember when we found those old ice skates? We waited all summer and fall for winter to come, so that old pond would freeze over and we could go ice skating."

"Yeah, it's a good thing that old pond isn't very deep. We would have drowned."

Roy said, "Yeah, that old pond would never freeze over thick enough to hold us up. I wonder how many times we fell through the ice."

"You know," Coy remembered. "It was really hard to walk through the mud to get out of that cold water with those stupid skates on."

Roy jokingly said, "Some folks think it's hard to walk in mud with rubber boots on. They should try it with ice skates on."

"Do you remember Dad saying he didn't think we would be able to have children, after the umpteen time we fell through the ice?"

"Boy, we fooled him didn't we?" Roy said, "Well, Bubba, the old house is gone but someone has built a new one.

Coy asked, "Do you suppose there are still bullfrogs and catfish in that old pond?"

"I don't know, but as many as we turned loose in there, there should be."

Coy said, "We did stock that old pond pretty well, didn't we?"

"Hey, let's go find out."

And with that the two boys walked down to the pond. When the boys got to the pond they found some of the biggest frogs they had ever seen. These frogs would probably weigh at least three pounds apiece. Coy said, "Roy, why don't we get four or five of these critters and take them home. Maybe the girls will want to try some frog legs."

"Ok, let's do it."

With that they found some small hickory tree limbs, small enough to cut and make spears out of them. Taking off their shoes and socks, they waded in to the pond and started to spear the frogs. After a short time, they had five frogs. They put their shoes and socks back on and started to go back to the truck. Roy said, "You know, we had better clean these frogs or they will go bad on us."

Coy said, "True. I wonder if that house has an outside faucet and if those folks will let us use it to clean these frogs?"

"Well, let's go find out."

The boys went to the door of the house and rang the doorbell several times. No one answered, and Roy said, "I guess there is no one home."

"Well, they probably won't mind if we use that faucet, so let's go around back and clean these frogs."

While they were cleaning the frogs, Coy looked up and said, "Hey, Bubba, look at that."

"Look at what?"

"That glass building back there," Coy answered.

"Oh yeah. Is that a pool in there?"

Coy said, "Yep, it's one of those indoor pools."

"Wouldn't it be a blast to go skinny-dipping in that?"

"Well, their ain't nobody here but us chickens, so they say in china," Coy replied.

And so the boys went over and tried the door. It was not locked, so they went in, stripped off their clothes and dived into that nice, clear, cool water. They were having a great time, when they heard a rumbling sound from outside. Taking a peek over the edge of the pool, they knew they were in big trouble. Parked next to the house was a car with an elderly couple in it. They were looking at their pool house.

In a state of shear panic, the two old skinny-dippers climbed out of the pool and streaked to Roy's truck, leaving their clothes behind in the pool house. They climbed into the truck when Roy screamed and jumped out of the truck. He ran back to the pool house to grab his keys out of his pants pocket. He threw his pants back down and ran back to the truck, put the key in the ignition and started the truck. As he was putting the truck in gear, Coy asked, "Roy, why did you run back to the pool house?"

Roy replied, "I left my keys in my pants pocket."

"Then where are your pants?"

Roy looked at Coy and said, "Oh no! I don't believe I did that. I threw them back down."

Coy said, "I don't believe you did that either. In fact, while you were there, why didn't you grab both our pants? We could use our wallets, you know."

About that time, a flashing red light appeared in Roy's rear view mirror. Roy pulled the truck over to the side of the road. Sheriff Bohan walked up to the truck and asked, "May I see your driver's license and registration please?"

Roy said, "I'm sorry, but I must have lost my license, sir."

The Sheriff smiled, "Could it be possible that you not only lost your license, but your clothes as well?"

"Well, I guess that could be a great possibility, now that you mention it."

"Let me see if I have this right," the Sheriff started. "The last time I saw you two, you were both covered with cow manure and you had a bucket, with a little milk, that also had cow manure in it. At that time you were trying to steal some milk, not the cow. Is that right?"

"Well, yeah, that would be correct."

The Sheriff asked, "So this time, were you trying to steal the pool, the water, or did you just want to show off your magnificent bodies to that old couple that have your clothes and your wallets? Oh yes, they also have your frogs."

Coy jumped in, "Sheriff, we didn't mean any harm. We just thought we would go for a swim. There wasn't anyone around."

The Sheriff said, "Well, Mr. Jackson wants you two to come back and get your 'crap', as he put it, out of his pool house. On the other hand, Mrs. Jackson wants you to come back and put your underwear on so that she can properly tip you each with a five dollar bill down the front of your shorts. I, however, am going to keep notes on you two. At the rate you two are getting into trouble, I am going to write a book, and it will probably be a best seller. Even though it will all be true, I will have to sell it as fiction cause no one will believe it."

With that, the Sheriff escorted the boys back to the Jackson house. Mrs. Jackson walked up to the truck and handed their underwear to both

Coy and Roy. She stood back and waited for them to put their briefs on, then held out two five dollar bills. She motioned for them to get out of the truck and walk to the front. As they did, she walked up, pulled the front of their briefs out and dropped a five dollar bill into it. As she did so, a newspaper reporter snapped pictures. Sheriff Bohan said, "Well boys, I guess I should have told you that Bill here works for the Oklahoma Tribune. He is riding with me today. He just wanted me to tell you that this is the biggest story he has ever covered."

Mr. Jackson, grinning from ear to ear, walked up and handed the boys their pants and said, "I put the frogs in your pant's pockets. I want you to know I ain't never seen such a sight in all my born days. If you think of something you want to do that's this funny again, please call us up and let us know so we can bring a camera next time."

As Coy and Roy were driving home, Roy said, "Coy, we are in really deep doo-doo this time."

Coy asked, "Is there anyway we can lose that paper before Virginia can read it?"

"There ain't no way."

As they pulled up in the driveway, Roy said, "Coy, look at all these cars. Were we having a party to night?"

"I don't remember anyone saying anything about one."

Roy pulled into the driveway. Maureen and Virginia walked up to the truck and waited for the boys to get out. Coy and Roy looked at each other and shrugged. As they got out of Roy's truck, a crowd of people including relatives, neighbors and what appeared almost everyone living in and around Oklahoma City, came out from behind the house. Maureen walked up to Coy at the same instant Virginia walked up to Roy. Right on cue, they each pulled the front of their husband's pants out and dropped a ten dollar bill down them. The crowd applauded and everyone started to explode with laughter. Coy looked at Roy and asked, "How did they find out so quickly?"

Roy said, "I don't know."

The whole crowd shouted out, "You were on TV receiving your tip and your clothes!"

Someone in the crowd yelled out, "You old boys sure could have used a body make over though. That was rough on our eyes."

For the next week, when Coy and Roy came into a room, both Maureen and Virginia would jump up, clap their hands, at the same time sing "Ba-bumpa-bump-ba-bumpa-bump," while laughing at how red faced the boys would get.

Things were pretty quiet for a couple of weeks. Maureen and Virginia decided maybe their husbands had finally grown up and gotten past the second childhood phase. In fact, one Saturday morning the boys were sitting at the dining room table, looking through the want ads. Coy said, "Hey, Bubba, here is an ad I am going to answer. Someone is selling a '40 Ford coup. I have wanted one of those for the last 54 years."

Roy said, "You should get it, Bubba. That's the same year you were born."

"Well then maybe you should go with me, because he also has a '41 Chevy coup for sale too. That's the year you were born."

Roy said, "You know, we should at least go and look at them."

Maureen and Virginia looked at each other and Maureen said, "Hey, if you can buy them, why don't you?"

Virginia said, "Sure it would be fun to drive around in them."

With that, the boys cut out the ad and headed out to look at these old cars. As they were going out the door, Coy turned back toward the girls and said, "Hey, if we get these cars, they will match our canoes. We will have to build some trailers to tow our canoes on."

When they arrived at the address, they found it was a small farm just a few miles outside Moore, Oklahoma. The farmer was an elderly man. As they were looking at the old cars, the old gentleman was telling the boys he had kept them up for a grandson. His grandson had decided he didn't want to be bothered with them. He was more interested in German cars. The old fellow said he wanted someone to have them that would appreciate them, as he had kept the cars in their original condition.

Coy said, "Well, we would really love to have them. These cars were built the same years that we were born."

Roy asked, "What would you sell them to us for? If we can get the money, we really do want them."

The old gentleman smiled and said, "Let's go have a cup of coffee and I'll get the titles for you. By the way, these cars have been souped up just a tad, so if you get to racing them, just be very careful. Don't total them because there aren't many parts around to fix them back up."

With that, he handed the titles over to the boys and said, "Just take care of them. Keep in mind, these cars are as old as you two are."

Both Coy and Roy said, "Yes, sir. We will."

The old man said, "Yeah, I'll bet you can't wait to race them. Go on, but come back and see me once in a while, ok?"

Coy and Roy called Virginia and asked her to come to this address and pick up Roy's truck and take it home. Coy and Roy got into their new old cars and headed out to the road for their trip home. Both of them were beaming from ear to ear.

After washing and waxing the old cars, the boys spent a couple of weeks just driving around in the country. They showed off their new found treasures and looked for drive-in restaurants, to relive the past. Maureen and Virginia loved it too. Both of the girls were making themselves a poodle skirt, looking for some black and white shoes and even growing their hair out for ponytails. Coy and Roy were growing out what little hair they still had trying to comb it into the D.A.'s of the fifties. They were wearing tee shirts, jeans and Penney loafers, trying to get back their youth.

One night, the four old teenagers were sitting at a drive-thru restaurant having their evening malteds, root beer floats and just chatting about some of the good old days. Roy asked Coy, "Do you remember the time we were racing from Sand Springs to Tulsa and then to Sapulpa? You, Wayne and Ray ended up in jail for eight days."

Coy said, "Yeah, it was quite an experience, as I recall. There was a large group of folks brought in later that night still in a party mood. The cell block was a steel structure inside a large concrete room, sort of like a barrel. This group of folks started to beat on the walls of the cell block, with a pretty good rhythm. They were singing and laughing, and we couldn't sleep. So we just joined in and started dancing and singing along. Boy, what a party! The jailers weren't too happy with us, but we didn't care. It was kind of funny. They not only didn't book us, they didn't even ask us what our names were. We found out later that our parents were looking for us. The same folks who locked us up had all points bulletin out on us, and these folks were all looking for us for eight days. Maureen asked, "Why were you put in jail in the first place?"

Coy said, "Well, it all started with six of us smoking cigars and drinking a couple of 2% beers. One of the guys had a meat cleaver in his car, and to make matters worse, when we stopped at the skating rink in Sapulpa, he decided to steal some hub caps while the rest of us were inside. We went to jail with him because we were in his car."

"After eight days, the police figured out me and Ray didn't know anything about all this other stuff and just let us go. We sure had some upset parents when they found out we had been in jail all that time."

Roy said, "Hey, Bubba. Let's take these fine looking fillies for a drive around our old racing loop, what do ya say?"

Coy said, "Let's go."

"Oh no," Virginia said nervously. "We ain't going to go racing with you two, are we Maureen?"

Coy replied, "Hey, I don't think anyone said anything about racing."

"Virginia, have you ever in our entire marriage or while we were dating seen me racing?" Roy asked.

"Well, no but there could always be a first time."

As they were getting ready to leave, Coy yelled, "Hey, Bubba what say on our way, we make a stop up on Brunner Hill and see if we can have our way with these fine looking old chicks."

Roy said, "Yeah, I think that's a fine idea."

Virginia yelled out, "I don't want to tell you two where to go, but it will be a lot warmer there than it is here." They all laughed as they pulled out on the road.

Later that evening, when the gang got home, Virginia said, "That was a pretty nice drive, wasn't it Maureen?"

Maureen said, "It sure was, and I really enjoyed the stop on Brunner Hill too."

Virginia said, "Well, I wasn't disappointed my own self, as they say."

The next morning, the gang had breakfast together, and chose to go to a water park for a few hours. Later that evening, Maureen and Virginia decided they would like to go to the movies. There was a new movie that they were just dying to see. It was a very romantic movie, the kind that makes most men cringe. So the boys decided they would rather drop the girls off and go for a drive.

After dropping off the girls, the boys stopped at a little diner for coffee. While they were having their coffee, Coy said, "You know, Bubba, that old Ford of mine is really a hot little car."

"Yeah, but my old Chevy is hotter."

Coy disagreed, "No, Roy. Chevy's have never been hotter than Fords. I mean, heck, I can remember when we were kids. Those old Fords I used to drive not only would run off and leave the Chevy's in the dust, but they also ran cooler. The engines didn't overheat."

Roy said, "Coy, you are so full of BS, It ain't even funny. That old Chevy of mine out there would just run off and leave your Ford so far behind, you wouldn't even be able to see the tail lights."

Coy asked, "Bubba, are you challenging me to a race?"

"If you think that old Ford is so hot, well, then yeah I am."

Coy said, "Ok, buster brown. Put your money where your pie hole is, cause I could use some more cash."

"Well, Bubba. Here is a twenty dollar bill. Do you think you can match it? Or do you just want to give me five dollars to forget what you said, cause you are afraid your old Ford won't make it."

Coy replied, "Hey, I tell you what I am going to do. I have $40 here that says me and my old Ford are going to be here, having my second cup of coffee when you and your old Chevy get back."

Roy turned a little red in the face and said, "Ok, Buster. You are on and $40 it is. Let's get it on."

So the boys went out to their cars. Coy said, "Ok, Bubba, here is some rules. We do need to be sort of safe about this."

Roy agreed, "Yeah, that's true, so tell me the rules."

Coy said, "No passing where it isn't safe. No passing when we coming into a town and we must slow down to the legal speed limit. We have to stop for red lights and stop signs, and we also stop for pedestrians. If only one of us gets caught at a red light, the other one has to pull over and stop 'til the red light changes, ok?"

"Ok, deal."

The boys fired up their cars and pulled out onto the highway. There was no traffic on the road at this hour, so the boys took off like a shot. They were side by side for close to a mile, until a set of head lights appeared in the distance coming toward them. Roy was in the left lane, so Coy backed off and let him pull back into the right lane.

Coy stayed behind Roy for a couple of miles just drafting him. Just as Tulsa was coming into sight, Coy pushed the throttle pedal to the floor and shot out and around Roy and his bright yellow Chevy. As soon as Coy passed the city limit sign, he released the throttle pedal and slowed down to the posted speed limit. Roy, however, shot around Coy, and his candy apple red Ford gained about a hundred yards. Then they slowed down to the speed limit as they approached the first stop light. Roy went through it on the yellow light, Coy stopped for the red light.

Roy pulled up to the second red light and had to stop. Coy pulled away from the first red light as soon as it turned green. He started to pace the lights. As soon as the second light turned green, Roy took off burning the rubber off his tires. Coy was still about a hundred yards behind Roy and still pacing the lights. Roy was coming to the last light when it turned red. Roy locked his brakes and skidded to a stop. Just as the light turned green, Coy was passing Roy and pushed the throttle to the floor. Roy slammed the throttle down, his tires were spinning but he was not gaining speed. He backed off his throttle, stopping the tire spin, then eased the throttle back down and roared off after Coy and the Ford.

Coy stayed out ahead of Roy all the way to Sapulpa. As Coy passed the speed limit sign, he slowed down to the posted speed limit. Roy, however, stayed on the throttle until he had passed Coy and gained a little distance between them. They were both pacing the stop lights. Just as they were coming up to the last stop light, it turned green and both boys pushed the throttles to the floor. The race for Sand Springs was on.

Coy and Roy both spotted the flashing red lights in their mirrors at about the same time. Roy was still in the lead and Coy was close behind, Roy however made a wrong turn and before they knew it, there was a Ford and a Chevy race going across the golf course. Roy was trying to find his way out of the mess he had gotten into, and poor old Coy had no idea where they were going. As they came over a little hill, Roy suddenly slammed on his brakes. Coy swerved to the right and slammed on his brakes as both cars slid into the pond. Luckily, it wasn't very deep.

The police pulled up, and using their public announce system, ordered the boys to get out of their cars, walk back to the grass and lay down on their stomachs with their hands out to their sides. The two old men sheepishly complied and were promptly hand cuffed and placed in the police car. The police officers got on their radio and called dispatch. They were laughing their heads off as they were telling everyone on the radio about their call, while asking for two tow trucks. After the boys were locked up in jail, they were allowed to make a phone call. After flipping a coin, Roy got to call Virginia and give her the good news. Coy could tell it was not going well when he heard Roy start pleading, "Wait. Please wait, my most beautiful wife. Don't be mad at me. It was Coy's fault. He made me do it. You know I would never do anything like this. I mean, I wouldn't even know how to race. I have always drove trucks and you don't race trucks. Please come to Sapulpa and bail us out. Please, pretty please."

Virginia said, "Well, we will think about it. We will have the cars towed home and you two can spend the night in jail. We will think about your bail in the morning."

The next morning, Maureen and Virginia arrived at the jail just in time for the proceedings. It seems the Creek County Sheriff, Sheriff Bohan, and a Creek County judge were at the jail to meet with the notorious Bozeman boys and to make them a deal they could not refuse. Judge Jones was the first to speak. He addressed Coy and Roy. "Boys," he said. "We here in Oklahoma have found our sense of humor doesn't seem to be as tolerant as yours. Our patience is somewhat shorter. Now Sheriff Smith would like to run you both out of the state on a rail, after a tar and feather job. On the other hand, Sheriff Bohan would like to hire a film crew to follow you two around 24 hours a day. It is his opinion that this great state would make millions of dollars just from the film royalties. However, Sheriff Smith seems to think the damages you cause could cost this great state millions of dollars, as well as some very bad publicity. Not to mention a lot of hard feelings with some people around here."

"So we have decided, if one or both of you would leave the state, it would be better for all of us. Plus, we would not look for compensation from either of you. Sheriff Bohan has stated if his book sells, he will offer you some small royalties. Now Coy Bozeman, I understand you normally live in Oregon. I would suggest that you go home, and if your brother would like to spend some time with you, maybe he could either go to Oregon or you both could meet in some other state."

"Now we here in Oklahoma wouldn't mind you coming back to visit, as long as your brother Roy went to Oregon to visit while you were here. So do we have an agreement or do we go to court to settle this matter?"

Both Coy and Roy were looking down at the floor nodded their heads that they agree to the terms. As they were leaving the jail, Maureen was saying to Coy, "Don't you think you and your brother could have as much fun just fishing, playing golf or sitting around a camp fire. You know, acting like older gentlemen?"

Coy with his head down said, "Well, yeah I guess so." Then he looked at Roy and said, But it sure as hell won't be anywhere near as much fun, will it, Bubba?"

Roy said, "No way!" They all burst out laughing.

That evening, all of Roy's children, grandchildren and great-grandchildren, came over for a good-bye dinner party. Coy and Maureen would be leaving the next morning to return to Oregon.

Chapter 9

The next morning, Coy and Maureen said their good-byes to Roy and Virginia. After a few tears and promises to get back together in Oregon, Coy and Maureen climbed into their old motor home. As they started down the street, they became aware of Sheriff Bohan leading them toward the freeway. As they proceeded along, it was apparent that other cars were pulling into the parade behind the old green motor home. There were lots of horns honking and people along the streets holding up signs saying 'Best Wishes' and other funny sayings.

Coy looked at Maureen and said, "It looks like some of these folks will miss us."

"I am sure they will," Maureen replied. "But, please don't think anyone wants you and your brother to do things like this again."

"Well, I suppose you're right. What do you say, let's do some camping and sight seeing on our way home."

Maureen said, "Now you're talking my language."

The Oregon couple headed out for more adventure. However, Maureen was keeping her fingers crossed. She was hoping it wouldn't be like it was in Oklahoma. The first day on the road seemed pretty dull, compared to their short visit in Oklahoma. They pulled into the campground for the night and enjoyed their dinner and coffee in front of an open fire. A fellow camper and his wife just happened to be passing by, looked over and called out, "Hey, aren't you one of those Bozemans from Oklahoma that was on T.V. the other night? You know, where that lady was giving you and your brother a tip for swimming in their pool nude or something like that?"

Coy's face turned red and he laughed sheepishly. Maureen laughed and answered, "Yep that would be my hubby alright." Within a few minutes, it seemed like everyone in the campground was sitting or standing around Coy and Maureen's camp fire. There were a lot of questions being asked and Maureen was laughing with glee at Coy's embarrassment.

Coy, however, didn't know which question to answer first, as they were quickly coming at him from all directions. After a few minutes of confusion, things calmed down and Coy discussed the situation with the crowd. He explained that he and his brother grew up in the country in Oklahoma. With His Dad being a disabled Veteran, there was never much money to do things. So he and his brother would seek out their own adventures.

On one occasion they lived in Cleveland, Oklahoma. The boys were on summer vacation from 1st and 2nd grade. It was a nice warm day, and their mother was washing clothes using some old metal washtubs and a scrub board. Coy, and his brother Roy, were probably the first hot tubers of their time. They dragged two of their mother's washtubs out to the well and filled them with water. They went into the house for a little while and waited for the sun to heat the water. They left their clothes in the house and streaked out to the tubs, climbed into the nice warm water and kicked back to enjoy their hot soak. They had been in the water about a half hour when Coy opened his eyes just in time to see the three neighboring teenage girls, climbing over the back fence. They were coming to visit with their Mom.

"Girls!" Coy yelled out. "Here comes some girls!"

He and Roy jumped out of the tubs, streaked for the house into their rooms and jumped under the bed. When the girls came into the house, they were laughing and related what they had seen while coming over the fence. In fact, they said it reminded them of elk. The boy's bodies were so dark and yet their little butts were so white. In the sunlight, it was almost blinding to them.

Ruth, the boy's mother said, "So that's why they were running so fast when they came through here."

One of the fellas said, "Come on. Do you really think we are going to believe that happened?"

Coy asked, "Why would I lie to you about it."

The fella said, "Well, I'm sure your mother had a washing machine."

Coy laughed and said, "At that time, she didn't have a washing machine. We didn't have electricity out where we lived. We used kerosene lamps and burned wood. In fact, our Mom cooked on a wood stove. Now, my Dad did find a washing machine for her the next year, though. It was a gasoline powered machine. Since Dad wasn't always around to get gas for her, He taught me to siphon gas out of his old truck."

"One afternoon, Mom asked me to get her some gas. I took the can and the hose and went out to the old truck. I probably swallowed a mouth full of gas, which by the way didn't taste very good. To add insult to injury, when I gave Mom the gas, my grandmother smelled the gas on my breath and promptly gave me first aid. She insisted that I drink a glass of vinegar to counter act the effects of the gas. For the rest of the day I kept burping vinegar flavored gas vapors. It was probably a good thing that I didn't smoke. I could have covered the whole state of Oklahoma in a split second."

A lady in the crowd asked, "Didn't your parents ever correct you and your brother?"

Coy laughed and said, "Sure, we got the belt of retribution every once in a while, along with the lecture about how, 'This is going to hurt me more than it hurts you.' I can remember on one occasion saying to my

Dad, 'I really don't want to hurt you, so why don't I just go on outside and we can forget this?' Well obviously, it didn't hurt him nearly as bad as he said it did, because it did happen as planned."

"There was a time that we lived in Bowden, when I was probably eight years old. I was out in the back yard and I found this old pad lock. The key hole was in the flat side of the lock. I wanted to open it, so I tried everything I could think of. Finally, I drove a nail into the key slot and clear through the lock. It still didn't open, so I pulled the nail out of the lock and put the lock in my back pocket. When I put it in my pocket, I had the sharp pointy part toward my backside. That hurt, so I turned it out away from my body."

Now I don't know why I went into the house, but there must have been a reason. As I came into the living room, I saw my Dad sitting in a chair reading a book. I could hear my brother and sister screaming at each other as I walked into the bedroom. This time I was absolutely innocent of any wrong doing. My Dad came into that room right behind me, grabbed me from behind, threw me face down across the bed and, with his hand, he started to hit as hard as he could on my backside."

"Now I noticed it didn't hurt, but I also knew that I had to have the proper response if I wanted him to stop. I was kicking my feet and screaming out in pain, even though it didn't hurt. All of a sudden, he left the room. A few minutes later, he came back into the room with a towel full of ice wrapped around his hand. He looked at me and said, 'This is one time it really did hurt me more than it hurt you.' Then he asked, 'What do you have in that back pocket?'"

A second Lady asked, "Coy, whatever started you and your brother doing these practical jokes and pranks."

Coy said, "Well, it was probably my Dad's brother. My uncle came to live with us when Roy and I were preschool age. My Mom told him we didn't have a bed for him, so he would have to sleep with Roy and me. He said that would be all right with him."

"At that time in our lives, my parents had Roy and me wearing bibbed overalls. You know the old farmer pants that had suspenders that went over the shoulders to hold your pants up. Well, my uncle went into the bedroom and drove two nails in the wall. When it was bedtime, he took Roy and me in to tuck us in bed for the night. I think it was about two nights later, Mom and Dad came to say goodnight and found us hanging on the wall like a couple of pictures. My Dad thought it was kind of funny, but My Mom was furious."

Maureen had baked cookies and made coffee for everyone, so the evening had passed by rather quickly. It seemed everyone had enjoyed themselves. Coy and Maureen were pretty tired after everyone had left and they decided to spend a second day in the campground to get some rest before going on. Coy was relaxing in the shade of the awning while watching the campers walk by. Maureen came out of the trailer and handed him a cup of coffee. "Coy," Maureen asked. "Did your Dad have a sense of humor like you and your brother?"

"Well, yeah," Coy said. "But sometimes his humor was a little painful."

"What do you mean by that?"

Coy continued, "Well, one afternoon after he came home from the war, I was probably around four or five at the time. I walked into the living room where Dad was laying on the couch smoking a cigarette. He called me over to him and asked, 'Do you want to see me blow smoke out of my eyes?' I said, 'Yeah,' so he sat me up on his chest and said, 'Watch my eyes.' I said, 'Ok,' and I leaned down and really stared at his eyes. Well he took a big puff on that cigarette and while I was looking into his eyes he stuck his cigarette in to my navel. I must admit, I did see a lot of smoke, but some how I don't think it came out of his eyes."

"A year or so later, after he had healed up and got so that he could get around better, he decided that Roy and I should learn how to fight. He would call us over to him one at a time and say, 'Put your hands up. I'm gonna teach you how to fight.' Being an obedient son, I put up my hands, and he kicked me clear across the house. Then he would say, 'Come back over here.' I would start to say, 'No, I don't want to play anymore,' but he would insist. I would walk back over to him and he would say, 'Now, why did you think I was going to hit you?' I would say, 'You told me to put my hands up to protect myself.' He would say, 'Ok. Put your hands up.' I would say, 'No, I don't want to play with you.' He would say, 'You had better put your hands up.' So I would put my hands up. When I thought he was going to kick me, I would try to block it and he would hit me upside the head."

After a few lessons like that, he would say, 'You boys come on over here. I'm going to teach you to fight.' We would just fall down on the floor, cover our heads and yell, 'We don't want to know how to fight! Go teach someone else.'"

"One time, Dad decided he was going to grow some cotton. He had bought a 160 acre farm in Mannford, Oklahoma on his G.I. loan. He hooked up his team of horses to a wagon, and took Roy and me with him to buy some cottonseed. It was an all day trip. On the way home it got really late and cold. Dad buried Roy and me up to our necks in the cottonseed and we went to sleep. When we woke up the next morning, we were still buried in the cottonseed parked out in the yard."

"Dad only tried to raise cotton that one time. He found out it was to much work. After the plants come up, you have to chop cotton. That means you have to take a hoe and chop all the weeds out of the rows. It was a lot of work for my Dad, because he would have to chop a row of cotton, then go and find me and Roy and drag us back to the cotton field. Then chop a row of cotton, then go and find me and Roy and drag us back to the cotton field. It was the same thing with picking the cotton, so Dad decided it was way too much work for him. Of course, Roy and I didn't mind Dad raising cotton."

After a good night's rest, Coy and Maureen started the trip toward home. As they were pulling out of the campground Maureen said, "Why don't we take the northern route home and go up through Yellowstone park? We could spend a couple of days there. Ok?"

Coy said, "Hey, that's a great idea."

So they were off to look for more adventure. A couple of days later they were in Yellowstone. The scenery was magnificent, but everything seemed sort of 'blah'. It just seemed like something was missing from their lives. While having breakfast one morning at the Yellowstone Lodge, Maureen asked Coy, "Honey, what's wrong?"

Coy said, "Well, I don't know. It's kind of like something is missing. The park is great, the view is beautiful, but it seems like something is missing. You know what I mean?"

Maureen said, "Yeah, but you know what it is? You and your brother had a wonderful experience going back and reliving your childhood, but it came to an end. Let's just have a good time, ok?"

Coy said, "Yeah, you're right. Say, did I ever tell you about the time, when we were living up in Cleveland, Oklahoma? I wanted to go fishing one morning, but my Dad decided I was going to baby sit, Roy and Barbara."

"No, I don't believe so."

"Well," Coy continued, "It was one of those nice warm summer mornings. I woke up early and went out to catch my mustang pony. That was quite a feat in and of itself. She and I had already gone through our, who is going to be the boss thing. She had to either buck me off, run under something really low to knock me off, or if all else failed, she would just lie down and roll over to get me off. She had to prove to me she was boss."

"Well, anyway, I had my fishing pole and can of worms. I was climbing up on my pony when my Dad came up. He said he and my Mom were going fishing. He wanted me to go down to the house, make breakfast for my brother and sister, and clean the house. I was to take care of Roy and Barbara while they were gone. I said, 'That's not fair! I was going fishing first.' He asked me, 'Who said life was fair?'"

"I started for the house, but I mumbled as I walked. He grabbed me by the shirt collar, jerked the bridle off the horse, and smacked my backside several times with those bridle bits. He said, 'That will teach you to cuss at me behind my back.'"

"So anyway, they went fishing and I went to the house. Needless to say, I was not in a good mood. When I got to the house, I fixed oatmeal for my siblings and sat it on the table. As I came into the living room, I told Roy and Barbara their breakfast was on the table. I started to clean up the living room, when into the living room came my little brother. He had his breakfast in hand and was dribbling a trail of oatmeal and milk all the way from the kitchen. I took that bowl from him and escorted him and his breakfast back to the kitchen table. I sat him and his bowl back down and told him in no uncertain terms he would eat his meal at that table. I had just started back to work in the living room when here came, 'Mr. I will do it my way,' back into the living room. Again, he was dribbling his oatmeal and milk along the way."

"At this point, I decided if I was big enough to watch them, then I was old enough to make them behave. So I went outside and cut a willow switch. I then came back into the house and applied the switch of knowledge to the proper area to make a correction. Well when my parents came home, my brother met them at the door and informed them about how badly I had beaten him. It was at this time I discovered that I was sadly mistaken about my age and my capabilities. For some unknown reason, I was old enough to be responsible for my siblings, but not old enough to keep them out of trouble. Therefore, I felt the wrath of the same willow switch that I had cut. I might add, the same switch my loving brother had saved for my Dad."

"Now my Dad would raise hot peppers in his garden every year. He did enjoy eating them. That night while we were eating dinner, I saw my Dad start to eat one of his peppers. I also noticed than when he bit into it, he instantly broke into a sweat and tears poured down his cheeks. He could not speak. I knew right away that I had to save that pepper. It must have totally surprised my Mother when I said I would do the dishes. I had to get my hands on that pepper, so I could hide it away for tomorrow."

"My Dad was taking a little trip and would be gone for a couple of days. The next morning came and I knew my brother would go into the kitchen when my Mom wasn't around. He liked to run his fingers through the sugar sack looking for sugar lumps. I took my pepper of retribution into the kitchen while everyone was outside. With a little water and a lot of sugar, I made a large sugar lump. I then went outside where everyone else was, and licked my sugar lump right in front of my brother. He wanted it so bad, so I let him strike a deal with me. If I had offered it to him he would have been suspicious, so I traded him out of his favorite shooter marble. He took that sugar lump and, just as I knew he would, put the whole thing in his mouth and bit down. He let out a blood-curdling scream. I knew I was going to get a beating for it, so I sure wasn't surprised. But at the time, I thought I was justified."

Maureen said, "That was a terrible thing to do."

"Yeah, you're right, but it was funny at the time. Besides, do you see this scar in the back of my head?"

"Yes," Maureen answered.

"Well, that's where Roy shot me with his bow and arrow later that same day, when no one was looking."

"Honey," Maureen said. "You and your family were nuts. But, it sounds like you all really enjoyed life. My family lived in town and we never had any excitement."

Maureen's cell phone started to ring about that time. As she answered the phone, Coy heard her say, "Well, Hi. How are things in Oregon?"

She turned to Coy and said, "It's Leah." They talked for a few minutes before Maureen said, "Just a minute, let me ask your Dad."

"Honey," Maureen asked. "Leah wants to know when we will be back in Oregon."

Coy said, "Well, today is Saturday. We should be home on Tuesday, I think. But I would like to go to the coast and camp at Bandon for a few days, I think. I have missed the ocean."

Maureen said, "Me too. Leah, your Dad said we will be back in Oregon on Tuesday, but he wants to go to Bandon and camp on the coast for a few days."

Leah said, "Then we will see you two in a few days, ok?"

Maureen said, "Ok, love ya and see ya in a few days."

The rest of the trip was fun but uneventful. As Coy and Maureen pulled into the Bandon campground, there were signs saying "Welcome Home. Coy and Maureen please follow the signs to 'A' loop. We will see you when you get here". Sure enough, when they came around the bend in the road, there were all their kids, grandkids and even a couple of great-grandkids. After all the hugs and kisses were out of the way, Leah said, "By the way, Dad, Uncle Roy called the other day and said he and Aunt Virginia would be here Wednesday. He said maybe you and him could have some fun out here. He said you will probably not have as much fun as you did back there, but maybe you could go fishing and play some golf. You know the 'stay out of trouble' kind of fun. What did he mean by out of trouble' kind of fun anyway?

Breinigsville, PA USA
21 March 2011
258123BV00001B/42/P